Letters *from an* Airfield

Letters

from an Airfield

THE TRUE STORY OF A GI BRIDE OF THE MIGHTY EIGHTH

JACK ROSENTHAL

First published 2009

The History Press
The Mill, Brimscombe Port
Stroud, Gloucestershire, GL5 2QG
www.thehistorypress.co.uk

British Library Cataloguing in Publication Data.
A catalogue record for this book is available from the British Library.

ISBN 978 0 7524 5252 4

Printed in Great Britain

In memory of my parents

'There's a silver lining through the dark clouds shining'
From *Keep The Home Fires Burning* by Ivor Novello/Lena Ford

Contents

Acknowledgements

The personal histories and much of the information in this book would have remained unknown to me had it not been for the help of people who gave freely of their time to answer my questions. They include Peggy Booth, Eileen English, Ada Frost, Agnes and Eric Goodwin, John Gower, Joan Hunting, Graham Hussey, James Jordan, Joyce Leek, Russell Ling, Herbert Meadows, Nancy Moore, Hilda Spoore, Bob Townshend and George Watson. Sadly several of them are no longer with us. In retrospect I hope my questioning did not stir any painful memories, as I now hope I have not offended with unwitting inaccuracies. Rather I trust I may have helped preserve recollections of hard but vibrant times.

My thanks too for the support and encouragement of Richard Holmes at UEA, to Bobby Rosenthal for unearthing family correspondence and to the Naval Historical Branch, Portsmouth and the Imperial War Museum for helpful responses to my inquiries.

Part One

East of Ipswich

At nine o'clock on an exhilarating morning of blue sky and glittering cold in late November 1910, Glencairn Stuart Ogilvie joined Graeme Kemp, his clerk of works, in the rear courtyard of Sizewell Hall. In view of the fine day the two men agreed not to trouble with car or trap but to walk the path that followed the low sandy cliffs above the beach to Thorpe Ness, that slight bulge on the Suffolk coast that puts it within a few yards of being the eastern-most point of Britain. Ogilvie was keen to inspect the full extent of the flooding affecting his coastal marshes after the week of gales and rain that had stopped most farming operations on the estate and had made the previous two days of shooting more trial than pleasure. More than that, he was fired with enthusiasm for a new project and was boyishly anticipating the effect its imminent revelation would have on Kemp.

Just south of the Ness lay a large brackish lagoon, the remnant of an estuary and anchorage previously known as Thorpe Haven. By 1910 it was silted and marshy, its opening through the beach to the North Sea blocked by sand and shingle which held back the water on the landward side sufficient, after winter rains, to spill it across the recently drained grazing marshes to the south. Scattered here and there on the slightly higher ground of the dunes behind the beach and on the dry heath to the north, black-tarred sheds and cottages of flint and red brick were inhabited by the handful of fishermen, shepherds and farm workers for whom the hamlet of Thorpe was home.

Ogilvie and Kemp stood on the dunes known as 'the bent hills' and took in the scene. Low in the south-east the sun laid a dazzling reflection across a calm sea dotted with small fishing boats out from Aldeburgh in search of sprats or cod. On the horizon to the north-east a procession of slow-moving brown sails and lines of coal smoke marked the passage of Lowestoft herring drifters returning to the fish quays after a night at sea. But Ogilvie's gaze was directed inland to where wildfowl were settling onto the floodwaters spread across marshes sparkling with frost. The whole view was treeless and, on anything but a glorious morning like this one, would have verged on the bleak. 'Kemp!' said Ogilvy, 'We are going to turn all this into a proper lake and build around it a model village!' His phlegmatic clerk of works was not altogether taken by surprise for Ogilvie had been putting in some groundwork over previous weeks and the estate staff had not been blind to the various well-dressed engineers and architects poking about around Thorpe. 'Whatever you do sir, it can hardly make less than an improvement.' Kempe replied. Thereon he returned to the estate office to begin marshalling his forces and within days, work began to install the sluices that would control the water levels of what Ogilvie had decided to call 'Thorpeness Meare'.

In this aspect of the project Ogilvie was fortunate in that his neighbour to the south, estate-owner Freddie Wentworth, had earlier drained his marshes by installing a new sluiced outlet to the sea which he now agreed could be used for the outflow from the Meare. The first effect of all this drainage work was that where wind-ruffled water had echoed to the call of coot and mallard in November, there lay, by the end of the year, a hundred-acre morass of mud and black ooze. This was bounded on its southern edge by a narrow causeway originally installed by Ogilvie's father, Alexander, to take shingle from the beach to the line of the Leiston–Aldeburgh railway link which the family firm, Brassey and Ogilvie, had built in 1859–60.

Alexander Ogilvie had accumulated a fortune as an innovative rail-way contractor and civil engineer and in 1859, having discovered the attractions of the Suffolk coast, he had bought the modest Sizewell House with a few acres as a holiday home and local base. Continuing success enabled him to purchase sufficient neighbouring property to create a 6,000-acre sporting estate which, after several unexpected deaths in the family, Glencairn Stuart was surprised to inherit in 1908. Stuart was inclined more toward the creative arts than creative engineering and, after initially studying law at Oxford, had involved himself in the London theatre world, enjoying some success as a play-wright. The plan he was now developing would provide an outlet for this creative leaning far beyond the estate's more prosaic rewards of shooting and farming.

The model holiday village he conceived would, taking the new Meare as its focal point, eschew contemporary architecture in favour of Swiss chalets, Italian *piazzas*, mediaeval manors and Spanish villas. The overriding ethos was that it should be a para-dise for children, a wonderland of adventurous discovery. With the important prerequisite of the children's contentment thus ensured, every delight would be provided for their relieved parents: tennis courts, a country club, a golf course, pleasure walks and flower gardens. Nor would there be any risk of disturbance from the normal seaside *hoi-polloi*: the development would seek as its cli-ents the best of London and country society, providing for them, should they not have their own, staff and domestic servants of the highest order. It was a bold and modern concept; but first there was the mud.

In the pious but often overbearing manner of the Victorians, Stuart's late mother, Margaret, had devoted herself to philanthropic works for the benefit of the district's poor. Perhaps influenced by her example, Stuart now struck on the idea of engaging fifty unemployed labourers from London to undertake the excavation of the Meare.

Much to the amusement of the locals this diverse contingent arrived at Thorpe Halt on his father's railway and, sporting a motley array of clothing, was marched off to an isolated house on the heath which had originally been built by Margaret as a children's convalescent hostel. Unfortunately within a week the bitter east coast winter and the physically demanding work had defeated the ill-clothed London men who were reloaded onto a train and sent back to the capital. They were replaced with a gang drawn from local fishermen and farm labourers well inured to the cold and wet.

One of these was William Goodwin, a tall and muscular labourer employed on the home farm of the Ogilvie estate and housed with his wife and young children in a tied cottage behind the beach just to the north of Sizewell House (by now enlarged and promoted to 'Hall'). Protected by thigh-high leather boots his job was to shovel the estuarial sludge into a 'tumbril', or tipping cart, fitted with wooden skids instead of wheels. When full it would be dragged away by one of the estate's Suffolk horses, great hooves slurping through the suction of the ooze. At nightfall William would return to his cottage caked in mud as black as coal.

Ogilvie was building the Meare to an imaginative design which used the excavated mud to form large and small islands which were then planted with willow and alder, both to stabilise them and to create secluded overhung channels connecting areas of open water. The plan was to encourage youthful adventures of voyage and discovery, much as Stuart had himself enjoyed as a child exploring the creeks and inlets of what had then been the old Thorpe Haven estuary. To enhance the youthful appeal Ogilvie called on one of his contacts from the theatrical and literary world, the master of childhood fantasy, J.M. Barrie, who was asked to approve the construction of various child-scale follies inspired by *Peter Pan*. 'Wendy's House', 'the Pirate's Lair' and the 'Smugglers' Caves' were concealed within the shrubbery of the islands, while life-size models of crocodiles and dragons lurked in the undergrowth beside the quieter channels. The creation could be fairly described as probably the country's first theme park. As work on the Meare progressed, construction of a large and ornate boathouse incorporating a clock tower and dovecote began at its eastern end, soon requiring Graeme Kemp to be despatched on a tour of the region's boatyards to find sufficient small craft to stock it.

On the dunes just to the north of the new boathouse, Ogilvie commissioned a timber clubhouse to be known as 'The Kursaal', a popular term at the time used to describe a cross between seaside hotel and colonial officers' club. This was planned as the social hub of the resort, to accommodate concerts and dances and provide an amenable environment for meeting fellow guests. It was opened with much ceremony on 25 May 1912, to be followed a year later, on 11 June 1913, with the formal opening of the Meare itself by Lord Huntingfield, the local representative of 'old money' and owner of much of the surrounding county.

Ogilvie had successfully utilised all his considerable contacts to attract the great and good of London society to these events and as a result received very favourable coverage in *The Tatler* and elsewhere in the upmarket press. The word spread; Thorpeness was fashionable and fantastically, where but three years earlier only a few labourers and fishermen inhabited bare heath, there stood a resort peopled by the well-heeled anxious to emphasise their status. Chauffeured cars passed to and fro at Thorpeness Halt as trains delivered visitors whose cultivated accents rang out over the Meare where previously only the wigeon whistled. With so much construction underway and plantings not yet matured, the project inevitably retained a raw and unfinished look, but nonetheless by the spring of 1914 all available accommodation was fully booked for the season with a waiting list for those properties still to be finished. It all looked very promising until in the middle of the season, on 4 August, the declaration of war inflicted an injury from which the scheme would never fully recover.

In the winter of 1910, as Ogilvie began his daring project at Thorpe, a traveller would have discovered TWO miles to the north-west another surprising development rooted in the Industrial Revolution and nurtured to fruition by the ambition of energetic Victorian engineers. Sited incongruously amid the quiet fields and ancient timber farmhouses where the sands of the coast meet the fertile wheatlands of Suffolk's interior, a small industrial town had grown around the engineering works of Richard Garrett. The son of a family of blacksmiths and gunmakers, the first Richard Garrett had come to the village forge in Leiston in 1778. Over the following century he and his sons had transformed this business from a small smithy providing farrier and tool-making services for local farms to an internationally renowned factory supplying steam-driven plant of all kinds to Europe, Russia, South America and throughout the colonies of the Empire.

The initial phases of this success stemmed from Garrett's early refinement of a reliable horse-drawn seed drill capable of planting in uniform rows, as opposed to the ancient methods of broadcasting or 'dibbling' seed by hand. Concurrently they had developed a portable threshing machine to separate grain from straw mechanically rather than by simply beating it with hand flails on the barn floor. Early in the nineteenth century the marketing of such machines received a setback in that they became a causative factor in the rioting of poverty-stricken farm workers who rightly saw them as a threat to their employment, and so began an intimidating campaign of cattle maiming, rick burning and machine smashing. Farmers were consequently nervous of investment in the new technology, but after the brutal repression of the rioters in 1830 they were less cautious. Demand soared and the manufacture of agricultural machinery moved from the province of the village blacksmith to that of the factory. The Garretts' location in the rich arable lands of East Anglia meant they had been well-placed to take advantage.

By 1910 'the Works' dominated Leiston physically, politically and psychologically, a fact impressed on the townsfolk periodically through the day by the shrill blast of 'The Bull', as the Works' steam whistle was known, which indicated the starting and stopping of shifts. At the latter signal the opening factory gates would release onto the High Street a surge of men and boys hurrying to the company-owned brick terraces of Mafeking Place, Kitchener Road and Waterloo Avenue; or to the pint glasses already lined up and filled on the bar of The Engineers Arms opposite. By 1914 Garrett's workforce numbered about 1,400 in a town with an overall population, including women and children, of just over 4,000. Should an imperceptive visitor wonder at the town's *raison d'etre* the clouds of sulphurous fumes drifting through the streets from the town-centre foundry would provide a noxious clue. Should they still wonder, the hissing of steam, the glow of furnaces and the clash of metal on metal would have left no doubt that here was industry forging commerce, wealth and employment to succour the Empire.

The success of Garrett's coupled with the feverish activity under-way at Thorpe meant that employment prospects in this corner of Suffolk were greater than those available elsewhere in the county, where low-paid seasonal activity on the farms or with the fishing fleet at Lowestoft offered the only opportunities. As employers, both Stuart Ogilvie and Frank Garrett were men of their time in that they combined a paternal concern for the well-being of their employees with a determinedly autocratic sense of their own authority, as evidenced by Garrett's dismissal in 1912 of a hundred or so men for suspected trade unionist tendencies. For his part, Ogilvie would drive about the district in his new Daimler with the chauffeur positioned, not behind the steering wheel, but in the passenger seat armed with a fire extinguisher with which to dowse anyone impudent enough to hinder progress by not giving way immediately.

William Goodwin's children needed no such dowsing to know that with their father an estate employee, they must not only avoid hindering progress should they encounter an Ogilvie, but show sufficient respect by standing aside with bowed heads. A particuarly rebellious daughter, Ruby, returning to Sizewell from school in Leiston, had once tired of this nonsense and catching sight of Margaret Ogilvie's horse-drawn sulky approaching from behind, hissed to her younger brother John 'I shan't take no notice; nor don't you!' The two children then walked on uncaring of Mrs Ogilvie's passing and determinedly refusing to meet her pointed stare. The result was that immediately on the sulky reaching Sizewell, William was called from his work in the fields to the estate office where he was warned that such insolence from his children in future would endanger his employment and thus his home. By the time Ruby and John scuffed up the sandy lane to their cottage door their father stood waiting, ready with warnings of his own.

Such overbearing behaviour from employers was not unusual at the time and was in any event eclipsed by the need to put a roof overhead and food on the table. Garrett apprenticeships were particularly prized, for despite binding the young subject to the company for a full seven years at minimal rates of pay, as well as requiring the deposit of a £10 surety – no small sum for a labourer to find – these indentures represented a security entirely lacking in any other available employment.

A mile south of Leiston is the village of Coldfair Green, or Knodishall as it is more usually called, where at the turn of the nineteenth century lived Charlie Thorpe, an agricultural labourer, with his wife, Alice, and two sons, George and Clifford. The family home was owned by Alice's brother Harry Lucas and was known as Mill House, though the old corn mill that had stood behind it had lost its sails when 'back-ended' by a gale in the 1880s and had subsequently been demolished. Charlie was a stout jovial man who cultivated a large vegetable garden and a bushy moustache that sweeping upwards gave the impression he was always smiling, which he usually was. Something of a foil to Charlie's ebullience, the tall and handsome Alice was weighed down by the difficulties of raising a family on a labourer's wages, the imprint of this struggle having soon dulled the bloom of her early beauty. On the floral-papered wall above the head of their shiny brass bed – a wedding gift from Harry – was fastened a cased barn owl. This pale bird, with its heart-shaped face permanently fixed in a vaguely mysterious pose of wide-eyed surveillance, seemed to represent the marriage of Charlie's calm serenity to Alice's practical ferocity.

On a morning in early June 1910, the family rose at five o'clock as usual, preparatory to Charlie and fourteen-year-old Clifford walking to Hall Farm to join four other men hand-hoeing cattle beet in Church Walk for tenant farmer Herbert Gildersleeves. Normally George, a year older than Clifford, would have gone with them, for hoeing was piece work paid by the chain and the earnings of one man alone were meagre, no matter how fast he worked. Should a particularly competent or ambitious hoer achieve an unusually large chainage in a day, Gildersleeves would walk the completed rows, head down in close inspection. Invariably discovering a missed weed or two plants too close together, he would mutter 'I shan't pay a full rate for a half job' and withhold part of the payment due. But on this particular morning George put on his best clothes, for Charlie had, through a well-placed friend at the Works, managed to secure him an interview with Ishmael Girling, the foreman of the wood-working shop, with a view to his gaining an apprenticeship. George, who had always enjoyed making things out of wood, possessed a diligent and respectful manner which was to serve him well. Mr Girling's impressions proved favourable and George was ushered into the main office for a brief audience before Frank Garrett who, after a few succinct questions concerning family background and work ethic, could think of no reason for rejection, and hearing none, instructed his chief clerk to bring forward a document of indenture to be signed by father, son and Richard Garrett.

After returning home to give his mother the good news and change into his working clothes, George joined the hoeing gang on Church Walk just before the midday break and excitedly relayed the events of the morning. He was to be signed as an apprentice threshing machinist to be trained in the making of the mainly wooden threshing engines for which the firm was famous and was to begin at the Works on Monday 26 June. One of the men congratulated him with 'Well, ye're made now bor; y'on't be doin' no more o' this sort o' work', which was the general feeling of all who learnt of his good fortune. The next seven years of his life would now be well-charted under the legally binding deed of indenture, not only between the working hours of 6am to 5.30pm, six days a week, but insofar as it required him to attend the company-sponsored Leiston Evening School at least once a week and to abstain from immoral behaviour, any form of trading, contract of matrimony, gambling or trade union membership.

Charlie and Alice were well content with this achievement for they knew that Clifford was not apprentice material and could hope for no more from life than the slight rewards of manual labour in the fields. They did not expect any great change in the arrangement of rural affairs and could not have imagined that events four years on would upset all expectations and render the document of George's indenture a worthless anachronism.

One person who in 1910 might have understood the inevitability of war was Frank Garrett. Since the 1850s the firm had enjoyed trading and manufacturing links with Germany – although not with the competing engineering business set up in Magdeburg in 1860 by Frank's uncle John after a family rift. In 1886, at the age of seventeen, Frank had been sent by his father to work and study for four years with the German engineering firm of Dehne in Halberstadt, the idea being to keep abreast of engineering and agricultural developments in central and eastern Europe, a region absorbing much of Garrett's output. On leaving Germany to return to Leiston in 1890, Frank was in no doubt as to that country's imperialist ambitions and carried home considerable respect for the well-organised efficiency of its industry and citizens.

Thereafter, as a matter of company policy, German nationals were employed at Garrett's in senior positions of sales and design. Machine tools were purchased from German manufacturers and steel was imported from Krupps. This slightly cosmopolitan aspect to the firm's workforce was further enhanced by the frequent despatch of trustworthy fitters, from the shop floor to far-flung outposts in Asia, Africa and South America, or wherever Garrett machines required commissioning or repair. Some of the more adventurous routes required serious provisioning as witnessed by a ledger entry for June 1869 which recorded the purchase of 'two live Berkshire pigs – food for Mr Baldry on the voyage.'

The Emigrants

As the seventeen-year-old Frank Garrett made his way to Halberstadt in 1886 he might have passed travelling in the opposite direction a German-Jewish father escorting his two youngest sons to Hamburg to embark ship for the United States. The more robust of the boys was twelve-year-old Siegfried Rosenthal, two years the senior of his rather shy brother Wilhelm. Their mother, Rosa, had died prematurely of tuberculosis, precipitating a pragmatic decision by their grieving father to entrust the boys, the youngest of his five children, to the care of the families of his two brothers in New York. These siblings had been a part of the great exodus of European emigrants that had crossed the Atlantic during the last decades of the nineteenth century, fired with the conviction that life in the New World would be better than that in the old. The boys' older brother, Emil, and two sisters, Toni and Bella, had to suffer the frustration of being denied an American adventure by respect for their father's wishes that they stay with him to help run the family butchery business and keep house in the little spa town of Bad Nauheim, thirty miles north of Frankfurt.

In New York Siegfried and Wilhelm lived with their uncles and aunts in the Jewish community of the Lower East Side. On leaving school Siegfried – known to all as Sig – found employment in the clothing trade. Wilhelm preferred the quiet study of chemical reactions which eventually equipped him with sufficient knowledge to enter the tanning and leather trade, and in 1896, aged twenty, he left New York for Pernambuco, Brazil as a procurer of hides. Sig matured into a man of energy in his field which narrowed to a specialisation in the design and manufacture of ladies' undergarments which, at that time, comprised a fuller range than is the case today. By the beginning of the new century he was in business for himself at 16 East 34th Street and was supplying many of the city's major department stores.

One of these was the *Surprise* owned by another German Jew, Arthur Geers. Geers was actually Geishefer, but Arthur's father had decided to Anglicise the family name on arrival from Europe. Arthur was more playboy than businessman, having spent much of his youth carousing up and down the country's west coast. In Seattle he had met and married compatriot Hilda Frauenthal whose father owned a successful department store in that city. When his own father died, Arthur returned to New York to set about dispersing the assets of the Surprise, initially by renting a sumptuous apartment on the Upper West Side where, on Tuesday nights, he and Hilda hosted poker parties to which Sig was usually invited. Here, on an evening in 1909, Sig, now thirty-five and a wealthy bachelor, was to win more than he could have anticipated.

Sixty years earlier another German, from Bavaria, had left his homeland with a young wife and hope for a better life in America. Louis and Sarah Landecker's arrival in New York from the east coincided with the arrival from the west of the news that gold lay ready for the taking in California. There was a choice of route: around the Horn by ship; through the deserts of Mexico and the south-west; or the direct way straight across the middle, taking railroad and riverboat to Missouri, then wagon train over the Great Plains, the Rockies, the deserts of the Great Basin and finally the High Sierras. Louis and Sarah decided on this classic route, survived its notorious hardships and eventually arrived in Placerville, California where they staked a claim, built a house and raised five children.

Placerville was a wild sort of place during the gold rush and was more often referred to as 'Hangtown' because of a tendency on the part of its citizens to summarily lynch alleged wrongdoers. Nevertheless as a 'boomtown' it offered plenty of business opportunities to a man of resilience and acumen and Louis was no sluggard on either count. Beyond developing his mine, he built and opened a general store, a warehouse and, at nearby Coon Hollow, a hotel for miners. He employed 100 Chinese labourers to collect the fibrous root of the soapweed plant which he processed as a substitute for the curled horsehair used to stuff mattresses, the demand for bedding having outrun the ability of the horse population to supply its main component. He soon became a notable figure in the young settlement and as such assumed the role of advisor and sometime guardian to another notable resident, but one on the slippery slope of alcoholism, James Wilson Marshall.

Marshall was a Scottish carpenter and something of a wild man, even before 24 January 1848 when, while constructing a sawmill on the nearby American River, he had spotted in the tail-race the gold nuggets which began the rush west. After his discovery Marshall had been forced off the site of the find to retire hurt, poor and angry. Occasionally in later years intoxication would result in his loosing off shots from a handgun endangering the rather unforgiving inhabitants of Placerville. At least once, when shots had come close to terminating the life of one or more taunting children, Louis's intervention was required to avoid things getting out of hand and the town reinforcing its reputation.

While Landecker was establishing himself in Placerville another fellow German, deciding to take what was perceived as the less hazardous route around the Horn, was shipwrecked off Chile and, after surviving for some weeks on barbecued monkey, arrived too late for the gold rush. He was, though, just in time for the new 'rush' which was for silver in Nevada, and so Moses Korn altered course for Virginia City in that state. Finding the mining of silver another unexpectedly hazardous undertaking, he sensibly realised that a great deal more money could be made selling whisky to the hard-drinking miners than by pick-axing in the hard rock of the mountains. He opened a liquor store in Gold Hill a mile south of Virginia City, prospered and married. A son, Isaac, was born in 1864 whereupon Moses and his wife Barbara decided that a liquor store in a frontier mining town was no place for a child of theirs and so moved to Seattle where they opened a new and larger retailing business.

After high school in Seattle, Isaac chose to study at the University of California's new School of Pharmacy in San Francisco. Graduating in 1887 he obtained his first position at a drugstore in Placerville, travelling first by train to Sacramento and then on to his destination by horse-drawn stage. At the drugstore he met Louis Landecker's nineteen-year-old daughter Carrie and on 18 March 1888, a week before her twentieth birthday, they were married. On the afternoon of the wedding day they departed on honeymoon to San Francisco aboard the first train to travel the new rail link to Sacramento, the ceremonial laying of the final rail having been incorporated into the festivities. After three days at The Palace Hotel the couple left San Francisco for the northern part of the state where Isaac was to continue his career as an itinerant pharmacist to the small settlements of the Pacific Northwest. In the absence of a doctor he would frequently be obliged to perform the duties of one, occasionally having to conduct, with minimal facilities, grisly emergency amputations on injured miners.

As a pharmacist, Isaac had learnt the Greek alphabet and joked with Carrie that they would have twenty-four children, one to carry the name of each letter. They wasted no time, for on 2 February 1889 a girl was born in Tacoma, Washington and was named Alpha. Something then went wrong for Alpha became their Omega as no more children were born. Yet one child was enough to engender Isaac's new name of 'Pop' Korn.

Pop was a relaxed, easy-going man who loved fly fishing for trout in the mountains, although this passion did once destroy his calm equilibrium by threatening his incipient alphabet. Aged eight, Alpha had persuaded her father to take her with him by train and foot into the remote depths of the Coast Range. Pop spotted a feeding trout in the fast water at the head of a pool and instructed Alpha to sit quietly on a rock while he stalked it. He manoeuvred into position, cast, scared the trout, and then himself when he looked back down the pool to see that Alpha had vanished, presumably having wandered off into wild country well stocked with rattlesnakes, mountain lions and numerous other hazards. Desperate calling and extensive searching revealing nothing, Pop decided to run several miles back down the railroad tracks to the station to organise a search party. This quickly got underway but darkness soon fell forcing Pop, sick with fear, to return home to break the news to Carrie. There he found

Alpha sitting at the table eating ice cream. She had been discovered wandering on the tracks by two railroad men who had brought her all the way home.

Alpha loved the outdoor life of the Northwest but grew to love art to an equal, if not greater degree. In Seattle her grandfather Moses numbered amongst his Jewish friends the owners of the city's largest department store, the Frauenthals, whose daughter Hilda came up with the idea that Alpha, now a teenage art student, might like to come to New York for an extended stay with herself and Arthur to explore the city's art world. Alpha adored New York. The Geers were well connected and she was able to meet many of the noted artists of the time, studying in Greenwich Village under the New York Realists John Sloane and Robert Henri. Henri advised her that as a woman she would have to choose between being a mother or professional artist – it would be impossible to be both. A decision was not long in coming.

Although Arthur Geers' failures in management were allowing the *Surprise* to slowly founder, he refused to abate his profligate lifestyle, continuing to throw lavish parties at the apartment as well as the Tuesday night poker games. Alpha, now twenty, would often help Hilda with the food and the drinks, which is how she came to meet Sig Rosenthal in 1909. They were married on 10 August 1910 and honeymooned in Europe. Sig later made a joke of their meeting, claiming that he had obtained his wife in a game of poker – by losing.

A Load of Barley

Mill House was, as the name might intimate, a surprisingly large property to be home to a farm labourer. Its main frontage looked east over Mill Road to the gorse of Knodishall Common with a rear wing enclosing, between itself and a range of brick and tile outbuildings to the north, a cobbled courtyard with an iron hand-pump cast at Garrett's foundry. A front bedroom was always kept ready for Alice's younger brother Harry who, for his part, was a surprisingly young man to be owner of such a large residence. The common view was that a goodly portion of the purchase funds might have been due His Majesty's Excise & Revenue in respect of items nocturnally transported to the cellar of the house from the beach below the gap in the coastal cliffs at Sizewell. This part of Suffolk had for at least two centuries been notorious for smuggling, and the Lucases held their own long tradition as seafarers and beach-men of resourceful independence. As a boy Harry had served his time on various sailing barges that worked the shallow waters of the east coast between the Thames and Newcastle and by 1900 he was skipper of the Ipswich-built *Marjorie*, a vessel primarily engaged in transporting corn and malt between East Anglian ports.

At the head of navigation on the Alde estuary three miles south-west of Mill House, Frank Garrett's great uncle, Newson Garrett, had in the 1840s, developed a maltings and corn merchant's business which was a frequent port of call for Harry. On such occasions, and when time, tide and the handling of his cargoes permitted, Harry would walk over the heaths and marshes of Freddie Wentworth's Blackheath estate to spend the night with his sister's family at Knodishall. He had bought the Mill House after the demise of the mill as both a security, in the event he should need a home ashore, and as a speculation, in that a Lucas was not the sort to deposit hard-won profits in anything so mundane or risky as a bank.

As youngsters the Thorpe boys, George and Clifford, were always excited to find that Harry had appeared at the house. Not only did he always have in his pocket a crumpled bag of aniseed balls but he also carried with him a great repertoire of dramatic tales involving shipwrecks, battles with excisemen and near escapes from death or marriage, which the listener might have felt Harry considered synonymous. These stories he rationed to one per visit, recounting them with great gusto and impeccable timing, inevitably pausing at critical points to slowly roll, lick and light a cigarette as the boys' hearts almost burst with anticipation of the next horror to be revealed: 'Go on Uncle, go on!' they would squeal as Harry lit up, raising his chin to the ceiling and inhaling deeply. Should Harry be returning to the barge on a Sunday, George and his father would usually walk with him, Clifford preferring to stay at home with his mother. By the spring of 1912, when George had been at the Works for nearly two years, a bigger adventure looked possible.

Dissatisfaction was widespread amongst the Garrett workforce that March, following the introduction of short-time working imposed as a result of the coal-miners strike that had begun in January. Garrett's employees were rural men isolated a long way from the centres of militant trade union activity, and were of a natural disposition to calmly accept their lot. Nonetheless they were possessed of a keen sense of natural justice and, in the main, a quiet dignity. The resolution of any sensitive situation that might arise was not at all helped by Frank Garrett's authoritarian attitude which now encouraged some of his more outspoken employees to bullish discussion of possible trade union membership. Whereupon an enraged Garrett sacked eighty suspected activists selected on the strength of rumour and hearsay as reported by his weasel-like wages clerk Lewis Chandler.

One of the sacked men was Ishmael Girling, still foreman of the threshing machine department and a Garrett employee for forty-six years. A man of great personal integrity and dignity, he had been dismissed for objecting to the manner of selection of those sacked. The whole of the threshing machine staff walked out in protest. This story of injustice subsequently made the national press, goading the furious Frank to decide on a total lock-out of all the men with effect from 4 April, which happened to coincide with one of Harry Lucas's visits to Mill House. Harry suggested that, rather than join his father and brother in the fields, George might like to sail with him down to Colchester in Essex and possibly on to London should there still be no recall from the Works: there was always the train if an urgent return was necessary. Although a few Garrett fitters might have travelled the world, and one or two men had been with the army in South Africa, most of the locals had never been further than the county town of Ipswich, and many not that far. In accepting what Harry now proposed, George felt that he might be entering that glamorous world of adventure his uncle had so often described when he was a child. On a morning tide the *Marjorie* left Snape quay on the Alde loaded with 120 tons of sacked barley for R. & W. Paul's Ipswich maltings.

Mayo

As Harry Lucas and George Thorpe navigated through the muddy shallows and sandbanks off the eastern-most shore of the British Isles, 400 miles away an Irishman in a sixteen-foot rowing boat worked the deep, clear waters off the western-most. At twenty-eight James Jordan held with his brother Michael fifty acres of poor land near Ballycastle on the north coast of County Mayo. But James was always happier in his boat than in his fields and here in the west of Ireland the sea was a good deal more productive than the land. Between outcrops of rock the peaty soil lies coldly saturated with the rain that sweeps across the bare moorland below roiling cauldrons of cloud driven in from the Atlantic on a relentless wind. Blue sky is rare. A still day most likely brings a midge-peppered drizzle that drips softly from the wild fuchsia lining the byways between the stone-walled fields and muffles the sound of the sea sucking at the cliffs.

More than with rain this land was drenched with poverty. Geology and geography had rendered it incapable of providing more than simple subsistence for a small population. Yet prolific childbirth and exploitation by a ruling class of absentee English landlords interested only in sporting amenities and rental income had conspired to create a painful legacy of famine and hardship. The brutality of the evictions prosecuted by the landowners during the Potato Famine had not been forgotten nor, before that, the cruel reprisals that had followed local support for the French invaders landing near Ballycastle in 1798, when avenging British troops had left many of the civilian population hanging from their eaves. It was a hungry landscape littered with relics of the famines and one almost synonymous with emigration. The promise of New York and Boston lay as the first landfall over the western horizon while closer to the east, Irish 'navvies' had built the infrastructure of Victorian England. As the emigrants would often recall in later years 'there was nothing there, nothing at all.'

James was not one of those planning to leave, for he had twin passions. One was the fishing. With Michael he kept cattle and sheep and grew oats and potatoes and cut turf from the bog for fuel, but it would all have been precarious without the fishing. The farm lay only half a mile or so from the cliffs of Downpatrick Head that rise vertically from the cold Atlantic where lobsters, cod and pollack abounded, free for a man with the means and the energy to take them. There was too, the burn that bounded the farm and filled with salmon after a late summer spate. Then, a short net surreptitiously fixed overnight to evade the landlord's bailiffs could yield a quick and profitable haul. Fishing at sea, though, was no easy vocation. First there was a walk of five miles to the nearest safe access at Balderry quay. A row of three miles then brought the boat back to Downpatrick Head where a turn to the north for another five miles brought the fisherman to the cod grounds. Here hand-lines jigged 150 feet below the boat could soon cover its floorboards with a knee-deep slither of fat, sea-green cod. But with deep swells rolling in on an unbroken fetch from Newfoundland, with Downpatrick Head a distant smudge on the horizon or, more often, obscured by mist and rain, a small open boat on a sea subject to sudden squalls was an acutely vulnerable place to be. This was why James and the other fishermen clung tightly to the superstitions of their trade.

No fisherman would talk of the sea with his back turned to it, nor blaspheme when upon it, for to do so would be disrespectful and invite its displeasure. Outward journeys always began with a quiet and solemn blessing of boat and crew with seawater. And for fear of outwardly acknowledging the truth that their survival was always a gamble, danger was always met with a covenant of silence. Should a stormy return passage require the jettisoning of a heavy catch, the inquiry of those ashore 'Did ye get any fish?' would be answered with nothing more than a stony 'No, nothin' at all', for stories of near disaster could only emphasise the risks and fuel apprehension amongst men and their families. Sometimes the truth could not be disguised, as when twenty-seven Ballycastle men were lost in a single night, drowned by a sudden storm that engulfed the fleet. Yet the prize had to be won for fish, fresh or preserved with salt, was an essential ingredient to survival when sold, bartered or shared amongst the family. And when it came to fish everyone knew 'Jimmy was your man'.

The other passion keeping James in Ireland was Catherine Langan of Ballycastle. Early in 1914 she agreed to marry him and later that year bore a child, Mary. As James and Catherine began life together on the farm, events unfolding in Europe reached even to this remote corner of Mayo. The Irish Home Rule bill passed through Parliament in September but was then suspended for the duration of the war. Hundreds of Mayo men signed up under recruiting drives for the Irish regiments of the British Army on the guidance of the leader of the Irish nationalists, John Redmond, who had vowed support for the British war effort on the basis that Ireland fought not for Empire but for 'the survival of small nations.' Most went for the adventure, and to escape unemployment. Others migrated to munitions work in England that paid two or three times the wages of any work that could be found in Mayo. Some – hearing rumours that conscription might be applied to Ireland – fled to the United States. Ironically some of these, falling on hard times, joined the US Army to eventually find themselves on the battlefields of France via an exceptionally indirect route.

In Dublin a breakaway group of nationalists led by Patrick Pearse sought to take advantage of Britain's wartime difficulties by staging the Easter Uprising of 1916. Their subsequent execution provided heroic martyrs to the cause of nationalism which, by 1918, was unstoppable. The threat of enforced military service in the British Army increased with the passing of the Conscription Act in April, fuelling a grow-ing wave of civil disobedience orchestrated by the radical nationalist party, Sinn Fein. In Mayo recruiting meetings were no longer viable as the lists of local men killed in France grew steadily longer and the horrendous stories brought home by maimed survivors gave the lie to the official line. Cat-calls and boisterous renditions of nationalist songs would thwart any attempt by speakers to present their case. In October a meeting in the town hall of Ballina – the nearest large town to Ballycastle – dissolved into chaos when an army band, called in to drown out the hecklers, deserted their instruments in favour of a baton charge of the audience. Within a month World War I was over, but two months later, on 21 January 1919, the Irish Volunteer Force, now renamed as the Irish Republican Army, had murdered two policemen in Tipperary and so begun a two-and-a-half year struggle against English rule.

In Ballina the IRA raided government offices and stores for arms and supplies and recruited throughout the countryside. Inevitably the feared 'Black and Tans' arrived in the district to implement their notorious campaign of terror and intimidation that, in Ballina, included the torture and murder of 25-year-old Michael Tolan, a tailor suffering from deformed feet. His body, minus feet, was found dumped in a bog outside the town. His feet were hurled through the window of his mother's house; she claimed £5,000 from the authorities in respect of his murder and received £750. Sporadic guerrilla actions continued. In Ballycastle an IRA ambush of a Royal Irish Constabulary patrol resulted in the wounding of two policemen and the death of a Ballycastle man.

A truce was agreed in July 1921 and was followed by the Anglo-Irish Treaty in December, but peace continued to prove elusive as civil war erupted between pro and anti-treaty factions. The 'Irregular' antis relinquished Ballina in the face of advancing Free State troops in July 1922 but retook the town with a daring raid on 12 September. On that morning, aided by an armoured car named 'The Rose of Lough Gill' commanded by a local Republican solicitor, a force of 150 Irregulars captured the Free State garrison and released fifty political prisoners before bombarding the post office and relieving banks and various other premises of cash and goods. Despite this plunder the Irregulars enjoyed the sympathy of many of the townsfolk and were well entertained before releasing the Free State garrison and withdrawing at 11pm. By the following spring it was all over as the Free

State asserted its authority and the leader of the Republicans, Eamon de Valera, ordered his men to lay down their arms.

Historic though these times were, James and Catherine were little affected by what in truth were only sporadic manifestations of the political turmoil engulfing Ireland. As farmer and fisherman James's life was governed not by nationalist idealism or British tyranny, but by the more immediate masters of season and weather with which he lived at close quarters. As is the desire of ordinary people every-where, he and Catherine went quietly about their business caring for farm and family. Another daughter Anne had been born in 1916 to be followed by two more girls, Agnes and Nora and then three boys, Michael, James and Jack. Jack was born in 1930, just three months before cancer of the colon took Catherine and left James to manage as best he could.

The children walked to school at the convent outside Ballycastle where they came under the strict tutelage of the Sisters of Mercy. Early in life Anne developed a rebellious fun-loving nature which inclined her to mischief at any opportunity. When she was ten she persuaded her six-year-old sister Agnes to join her in spending the day hidden under the road bridge near the convent to avoid school and the Sisters, who Anne regarded as more tyrannical than merci-ful. Agnes remembers the endless hours of damp, crouched silence as the longest day of her life. When she was sixteen Anne crept from her bed to the yard late one summer night and arranged a sheet over her head. After knocking loudly but dolefully on the front door of the house to summon its sleeping occupants she danced a slow-motion simulation of a phantom so successfully that her siblings ran screaming back to their beds leaving their superstitious father star-ing in disbelief and very possibly traumatised considering his recent bereavement. Surprisingly both escapades passed without discovery of their perpetrator.

More conventional entertainment was hard to find although there was the annual excitement of the Ballycastle fair held on a rough field known as 'The Banks'. The focus of attention was the horseracing which engendered much jovial bragging and degrees of intoxication as wagers were won or lost. At other times a gathering for a wake or wedding would bring out the fiddles and b'rans but, on the land at least, the overriding tenor was one of unrelenting physical work with little time or energy left for much else. The genuine phantoms of eviction and starvation were too recent to allow it. A yellowed photograph from the 1920s showing the seven Jordan children standing loose-limbed with their father in front of their modest home could easily be mistaken for the classic image of work-worn homesteaders marooned on the plains of the American Midwest.

The demographics of Irish family life were well established. At sixteen the oldest child would leave home to work away, often abroad, where earlier emigrants would have arranged employment and accommodation. Sometimes it could seem as if whole groups had been exported wholesale when young adults from some remote village found themselves still together but in Chicago, Boston or Kilburn. Such money as could be saved was sent home where the next eldest would have taken over as carer and helper to younger siblings. In the absence of their mother James's daughters carried a particular responsibility which is perhaps why, at first, all stayed close at hand. The oldest, Mary, who was sixteen at the time of her mother's death, took live-in domestic work with the Sisters of Mercy at the Ballycastle convent, as did Agnes six years later. Anne, mid-way in age between the two, had little time for nuns and found work in a private Ballycastle house. This brought her into contact with one of the network of domestic agents that operated throughout Ireland recruiting girls for domestic service in England. Tired of the convent, Mary had already left for London when Anne, on receiving a written offer of employment from Lady Frances Tufnell in Hatfield, followed suite.

Lady Frances liked her maids to be spirited and so was well pleased with Anne. So much so that she recommended the family to her sister Lady Constance who, in due course, wrote to Agnes at the Ballycastle convent inviting her to join her household in St Albans. Leaving her rather sickly younger sister Nora at home to help with father and brothers, Agnes arrived in St Albans in 1938 after Lady Constance had sent the train fare. Anne, who had by now been in England some two years, delighted in her sister's astonishment at the rush and clatter of urban life. The two young women spent most of their free time together, cycling to assignations with suitors or simply exploring their new environment, but in the spring of the following year Anne announced that during August they would not be able to see each other: Lady Frances had asked Anne to accompany the family on a month's holiday to what she termed 'rather a splendid new sea-side resort' – Thorpeness.

Woodmere

2,000 miles west of Ballycastle two other motherless emigrants, Siegfried and Wilhelm Rosenthal, were not so much sending money back to their family in Bad Nauheim as piling it up very successfully in their own accounts. Sig had briefly cornered the market with a particularly fashionable style of silk undergarment which brought an avalanche of orders and money to his 34th Street workshops. Within five years of their marriage he and Alpha had moved from New York City to a grand house close to the sea in Woodmere, Long Island. The beautiful Alpha, fifteen years Sig's junior, had become an elegant social hostess and also, by mid-1916, mother to three boys; Laurence, Edwin and Robert.

Robert was not the only new family member to arrive in Woodmere in 1916. After twenty years of silence Wilhelm re-appeared from Brazil crowned with startling white hair – the result of yellow fever – and a great deal of money made in the leather trade. On his homecoming the first action of this tall, broad-shouldered man of forty was to fall in love with his brother's wife and move into their spacious Woodmere residence. Here, in between weekly visits to the city to manage his money and a vigorous keep-fit program of cycling, walking and swimming in Woodmere Bay, 'Uncle Willy' took on the role of labourer for Alpha's artistic garden projects. Standing in the morning sun amid the flower borders, his tanned face match-ing his unvarying bachelor's uniform of brown shirt, brown trousers and huge brown shoes, he resembled a mountain with a capping of snow. He worked slowly but purposefully, hands firm on the shaft of the spade he handled as if it were a teaspoon. Fridays he went to the city, returning from the banks and brokers of Manhattan in the evening always bearing gifts; toys or candy for the boys, cartons of Lucky Strike cigarettes and 78rpm records of Caruso for Alpha. She ended up with the complete works.

Sig, deciding that he could grow a thing or two himself, cleared a small patch of ground and indulged a fascination with peanuts which proved a great success, amazing everyone, except perhaps Willy, when he later forked from the soil roots bedecked with masses of the little waisted shells. For Sig, peanuts were a symbol of the New World. From the outset of his life in New York he had been determined to endorse everything American and, being not in the least sentimental or nostalgic, had no inclination to recall, let alone celebrate, his German-Jewish inheritance. He agreed wholeheartedly with Teddy Roosevelt's dictum that 'there should be no hyphenated Americans'. This became something of a family joke in later years when Sig's instructions to his sons on matters American were intoned with his strong German accent still intact, but was no bad policy at a time when anti-German feeling was running high in the US prior to the declaration of war on Germany in April 1917. And vindication of a sort occurred on the Queensborough Bridge late one afternoon in the spring of that year.

Sig, Alpha and the boys were returning from a visit to the Geers at their West Side apartment in the big canvas-topped Marmen car Sig had recently bought. At the bridge they encountered a jam of cars and trucks embroiled in a chaos of wailing sirens, patrol cars, fire-trucks and even soldiers with fixed bayonets. The unpleasant, eggy smell of burnt gunpowder leant credence to the rumour, shouted back from car to car, that German sympathisers had attempted to blow up the bridge. Sig, always forceful, remonstrated with the policeman blocking his way: the boys had to get home to bed. It might not have been his German accent that prompted the officer's decision to unholster his pistol at that particular point in the discussion, but in any event Sig retreated back to the Geers' apartment for the night.

After the boys had been put to bed and a few calming scotches consumed, the conversation developed around the desirability of changing the name Rosenthal to something less Germanic, so as to avoid any social or business difficulties in the current political climate. After all, Sig's two uncles, the families he had lived with thirty years earlier, had changed theirs to Rhodes on arrival in America, and the Geers had been Geishefers. Alpha favoured Ross but, surprisingly for someone so willing to forget his roots, Sig would have none of it. Instead he made a show of his loyalties the following year by deciding to volunteer for US Army service. Sensibly, he left that decision until the war was in its closing stages, which was just as well or he might have found himself in arms against his elder brother Emil who was serving as a quartermaster in the German Army.

Alpha was much faster off the mark, volunteering herself and the Marmen for the US Army Motor Corps immediately war was declared. Larry had begun school, one-year-old Robert was left in the care of his nurse and Eddie accompanied his mother on official duty in the Marmen. Dressed in a pressed uniform of blue and grey, with red insignia on the cuffs, collar and stylish cap, Alpha made a glamorous sight speeding along in the polished open-topped car with the head of her three-year-old son barely visible in the passenger seat. Her job was to assist in providing transport services to the various army camps on Long Island that acted as staging areas for troops embarking for, or returning from France. Her good looks enhanced by her relaxed Western style made her a popular figure in the camps as she handed out cigarettes and occasionally invited small groups of wounded returnees back to the Woodmere house to enjoy a break from the harsh military environment.

Eddie was awestruck one afternoon at the appearance in the drawing room of a man missing a leg. Fascinated, he wanted to know all about the war. The soldier wanted to talk about anything else but Eddie persisted with innocent questioning. Suddenly the traumatised soldier was overwhelmed and could not hold back tears. Eddie was astonished – he had never seen an adult cry before and until that moment had no reason to believe that they ever did. It left a lasting impression.

Alpha's support of the war effort was not confined to the Motor Corps. In an effort to boost gold reserves the government had asked that any remaining gold currency held privately be surrendered for modern cash. Alpha had a bag inherited from her grandfather, Louis Landecker, after his death in San Francisco in 1900: $50, $20 and $10 coins. Unlike her husband, Alpha was an artist, sentimental, emotional and nostalgic: she did not want to let them go. They had been her private security ever since she had arrived in New York as a girl but more than that they were a reminder of the happy outdoor childhood she had spent in the West. She took them to the bank in Woodmere and on the way home Eddie discovered that grown-up women could cry too.

Willy's gardening was to provoke another unexpected situation the following week when Alpha's maid Katie, dressed in a formal blue and white uniform, came in from the garden to the kitchen where Alpha was arranging flowers. 'You should be ashamed of yourself!' she screamed at Alpha. 'Mr Willy does all the hard work in the garden. The poor man!' Sensing that something had tripped in Katie's mind, Alpha's decision was to telephone Captain Lynch at the Woodmere Police Department. Glad of an incident on a sleepy mid-week afternoon, and lacking any training in sensitive approaches to mental disorders, the captain arrived in his squad car with lights and siren full on and took Katie away. Which seemed an extreme reaction to a moment's insolence, but Alpha had correctly perceived that Katie could be dangerous. This became clear some months later when, after absconding from a mental institution, she returned to the house late one night armed with a large knife. Thwarted by finding all the doors and windows locked she took up a position at the far end of the garden where Willy found her in the morning and managed to disarm her without injury to anyone. Captain Lynch returned, lights and siren blazing again, and took her away for a second and, thankfully, final time.

More danger was afoot at Thanksgiving when the Geers with their daughter Peggy, six months older than Eddie, joined the Rosenthals in Woodmere for the celebration. At that time it was traditional for children to wear masks at Thanksgiving as well as at Halloween. Wearing his and showing off to Peggy with a bold plan to terrify any motorists who should pass by on the quiet suburban road outside, Eddie misjudged and walked into an oncoming vehicle. Peggy ran back to the house to appear in the dining room where the adults had just been seated as Alpha began to carve the turkey (the kitchen, the dining room and all things culinary stayed firmly in her hands). 'Eddie's been run over and killed!' she wailed. Before the horrified assembly could get to the front door the next-door neighbour, Mr Cheshire, came through it leading the fatality by the hand; a dazed and dishevelled Eddie with a bruised cheek.

In 1917, at the age of only fifty-three, the easy-going fisherman and pharmacist 'Pop' Korn died prematurely of diabetes. After that Carrie made frequent extended visits 'back east' to her daughter and grandchildren on Long Island where, for some reason, to the three boys she became known as 'Meema'. Her relaxed, outgoing Western style was even more pronounced than Alpha's, making her a popular addition to the household. Her detailed, first-hand accounts of gold rush days in Placerville, and of an adventurous life in the mining and logging camps, held the children spellbound, particularly Eddie who, more than his brothers, had inherited Alpha's bohemian spirit in far greater measure than Sig's Germanic discipline.

George and Florrie

By the early afternoon of Thursday 11 April 1912 the north-east breeze had increased to a gusty upriver wind making hard work for the two men and a boy working the *Marjorie* down from Snape against the last of the flood tide. The first reaches below the village are no more than a narrow tidal creek winding through the saltings; the inexperienced or unwary skipper of a deep-laden barge powered only by sail would soon find it stuck fast in the mud. Harry Lucas stood at the wheel, periodically calling instructions for'ard to Hordie, the mate, to 'leggo' the foresail or trim the mainsail as the vessel tacked a tortuous route between the 'withie' sticks marking the channel. Shoulder to shoulder with Hordie, George worked the lee-board winches or hauled on the sails, glad to keep his blood flowing in the chill wind.

Clearing the promontory of Iken church the worst was behind them as the estuary opened into the wide reach overlooked from the north by the square, brick mansion of the Wentworth's Blackheath estate, its pheasant-stalked lawns wrapped round by the home coverts, the swathes of birch hazel purple with swelling buds. The northeaster chased in from the sea under a blue sky unblemished by cloud, pushing up a chop as the tide began to drain eastward. Squinting-bright clarity was honed pin-sharp as the *Marjorie* drove her curling bow-wave steadily towards Aldeburgh, the bulging brown canvas of the topsail stitched with the white windmill cross that marked her as belonging to the fleet of R.& W. Paul, Malsters & Millers of Ipswich.

George was naturally a lad of gentle and passive character but as he worked the winches or watched the passing river traffic he felt an unusual elation. It was not just the fineness of the spring day, nor the passion sea-going men have always felt as decks under their feet begin to move to the motion of open sea. Nor was it the promise of travel and adventure, though that was exciting enough – he had never been more than ten miles from Knodishall – but, more than any of those, it was the realisation that he was beyond his mother's grasp. For Alice had remained a Victorian matriarch, upright and industrious, but controlling, ruling her household with a stern intolerance born of viewing life as penance not pleasure. Now, standing braced against the mast of the *Marjorie* with the wind in his face, George, for the moment at least, was free.

Passing the 'Brick Dock' that served the Aldeburgh brickworks the *Marjorie* approached Aldeburgh on a tide alive with sail despite plentiful evidence of the advance of steam power. The black hulk of the abandoned sailing trawler *Iona* lay marooned on the saltings where a storm tide had left her. Close by on the mud, neglected and without rigging, lay two of the old Aldeburgh cod smacks that through winter months had fished distant Icelandic waters under sail power alone. The last of them to be still working, the *Gypsy*, lay alongside Slaughden quay, home from a long-lining trip north.

The age of steam it might have been but in the years before World War I the coastal sailing barges were at the zenith of *their* age with almost 2,000 of them working the east coast from Yorkshire to Kent. Drawing only about six feet laden and flat-bottomed they could 'take the ground', that is stay upright, on mud or sand beside any 'hard' exposed at low water, thus enabling discharge direct into horse-drawn carts pulled alongside, while their shallow draught allowed them access to the lacework of tidal creeks and channels threading the hinterlands of the flat East Anglian coast.

Most villages anywhere near an estuary had a dock or quay where the commodities of trade such as coal or corn could be landed or loaded. Farmers would simply dig a barge-sized cut into an accessible part of the saltings where a vessel could lie to be loaded high with a deck cargo of hay or straw for the London horse trade. High tide would lift her off and the 'stackie' would set off for the Thames, a floating hay-stack with the mate perched atop the load relaying steerage instructions to the skipper at the wheel whose view ahead was of nothing but a wide wall of hay or straw.

At sea leeboards hinged on both sides of the hull were let down to act as keels. Heavy-laden and low in the water, big seas would sweep over the decks, but with hatches well-battened most of the sailing barges were sea-worthy craft allowing routine crossings to Holland or France. Coal from the North, coke from gas works, corn and straw from the farms, shingle from the beaches, malt, lime, bricks, abattoir waste to the glue factories, maize offloaded from the big clipper ships; the sailing barges moved it all. Powered only by the wind and sailed by a crew of just two men who were paid only when moving a cargo, they did their owners well.

Although the River Alde comes within a few yards of the North Sea at Slaughden just south of Aldeburgh, the confluence is denied by a shingle bank that, built up by the northerly longshore drift, turns the river ninety degrees to the south and keeps sea and river parallel, but apart, for ten miles until they finally join in a foamy tumble of tide-rips and shoals at Shingle Street. Now, with a following wind filling her sails and her sheets let free, the *Marjorie* was bowling southward, Harry intent on negotiating the hazards of the river mouth before the ebbing tide made the passage too risky.

As the circular bulk of the Martello tower – built to repel Napoleonic invaders – fell astern, the twelfth-century keep of Orford Castle loomed ahead. Holding to her line through the clutter of smaller fishing boats and ferries busy around Orford quay the *Marjorie* was soon slicing through the narrows beside the bleak flatness of Havergate Island. Harry raised his hand from the wheel to the solitary figure of Bob Brinkley the marshman who, a spade over his shoulder, stood on the low river wall watching the barge pass. Bob raised a straight arm above his head in an emphatic return salute, glad of any sort of communication, for he lived a lonely life on the windswept island, housed in a small brick cottage, watching over grazing cattle in the summer, fishing and wildfowling in winter.

Ahead, below the straggle of cottages looking east from the top of the beach at Shingle Street, a jagged white line of breaking waves marked the beginning of open sea. Despite the fast-flowing ebb the *Marjorie* began to roll with the swells pushing into the river mouth. Harry, bracing himself against the wheel, took her in close to the beach, lining up for the run out through the channel that moved with every storm. With an upward glance at tightened sails he spun the wheel to bring the navigation marks into line and the *Marjorie's* bow swung east. Incoming waves curled onto the submerged banks, breaking into a chop and churn of foam close on either side of the vessel as she surfed out into safety offshore and set a course for Harwich and the Ipswich River.

That night they anchored off Pin Mill in the River Orwell below Ipswich and took the ship's boat onto the hard beside The Butt and

Oyster. *The Butt* was popular with the barge and lightermen for much of their work involved loading and unloading the big clipper ships that proceeded no further upstream than the nearby anchorage in Butterman's Bay. George was accustomed neither to beer nor the boisterous repartee of the bargemen, for the atmosphere of Garrett's woodworking shop, although sociable and good-natured, was imbued with the quiet respectability of industrious work as inspired by its upright Christian foreman. Seated amongst motley beer-swilling seafarers in the smoky snug of The Butt, George felt that he had already travelled a long way from home. With the darkness the wind had dropped and the *Marjorie* rode quietly on the ebb tide streaming past her bows as the three men skulled out to her in the moonlight. The movement of the deckboards above George's berth that night had less to do with wind and weather than with the Adnams stout his senior crewmates had pressed upon him.

The morning flood took them up to Ipswich and by midday they had 'locked into' the wet dock and lay alongside Paul's wharf, the cranes busy hoisting ashore their cargo of sacked barley. Harry was booked to take the *Marjorie* to the Thames with malt for the London breweries late the next day, Saturday, but suddenly George's expectation of seeing the capital for the first time was crushed by the approach along the dock of 'Bluey' Gillett, the skipper of the Paul's barge *Thalatta*. Following on behind the *Marjorie* with another load of barley from Snape, the *Thalatta* had sailed on the night tide and had just come alongside the wharf. 'You the Thorpe boy?' asked Bluey, and at George's nod 'Ye're to go back. Yer father come down ter Snape in a latha yesterdee arternun an' says all th' apprentices is to be back at the Works fust thing Mundee.' It seemed the adventure was over: George knew that absence was not to be contemplated for, under the strict regime of Frank Garrett, dismissal would more than likely be the penalty under the legally-binding terms of his apprenticeship.

On leaving a vessel for home many hard-pressed east coast seamen walked the coastal paths from the main ports back to their villages but, as a skipper for Paul's, Harry had steady work and decent pay so felt the least he could do was to furnish nephew George with the train fare home to Leiston. After a second night on the barge, and a second attempt to master beer during an hour or two spent with Harry and Hordie in The Wherry, George walked up to Ipswich station from the docks and boarded the Lowestoft train.

The carriages were crowded with weekend travellers but George found a single seat next to a young woman accompanied by her mother. They didn't talk, for both were shy and George was aware that, after forty-eight hours in the same clothes on board a barge, he was not at his best. As the train approached Saxmundham and the junction for the Leiston line, the two women began to gather themselves to leave. The girl was very slight and George, who was also preparing to leave the train, reached above her to help lift her bags from the overhead rack. On the platform they found themselves waiting together. George tentatively inquired of the daughter if she was going to Aldeburgh. Her mother, friendly but perceptibly protective, answered that they were travelling only as far as Leiston as they lived at Highbury Cottages, about half a mile out of the town towards Saxmundham. George knew exactly where that was, as the road from Knodishall Church to Leiston passed in front of the terraced row built in the 1870s by grocer Robert Sawyer and named after his wife's London birthplace. Learning that the ladies intended to walk from Leiston station, George volunteered to accompany them to help with the bags as it was 'not much further to walk that way to Knodishall'.

With introductions achieved they sat together on the train and, like people inching onto creaking ice, slowly released personal details. The girl's name was Florence Miller, she was twenty (nearly four years older than George) and the only child of her mother Laura. Both were in service to the Honourable William Vanneck at The Cupola, his Leiston house, and had gone to Colchester the day before, their day off, to visit Florence's aunt. In the months ahead George was to learn that the two had come to Leiston from Wivenhoe in Essex where Laura had been cook at the big house in Wivenhoe Park. Years later he was to learn that Laura's pregnancy had not begun in the servant's quarters but at the other end of the house. To avoid embarrassment a marriage had been arranged to the estate groom, Mathew Miller. Eighteen years on, and suspecting her ageing employer might not hesitate to repeat the performance with his child, Laura had left Wivenhoe for Leiston, but without Mathew who, feeling he had more than fulfilled his obligations, preferred to stay with the devil he knew.

George walked with the two ladies, carrying their bags to Highbury Cottages and, on taking his leave, asked if he might call by at some time when it was convenient. Despite his relative youth, he was very taken with the shy, petite Florence whose nature seemed to mesh so well with his own. That summer, hurrying up the hill past Knodishall Church and the gloomy dank of Peggy's Pond, he would bring Florrie bouquets of wild flowers plucked from the roadside and on weekend afternoons, when she was not at work, the two would walk out together across the fields or into the town.

Entertainment possibilities in Leiston, like so much else in the last years of peace before World War I, were on the cusp of change. Earlier generations had made do with an annual works outing to the coast, an occasional tea party at the vicarage and the odd classical recital in the Works Hall; all fairly subdued affairs organised under the auspices of a patronising local establishment. This paucity of popular entertainment was not, in any event, readily perceived in an age when the time available for recreation was negligible and the struggle for survival – economic and physical – demanded unrelenting attention. For many of the men the public houses were the respite of choice, and there was always the sea for bathing in summer and fishing in winter. Every December Coldfair Green, as its name suggests, had been the venue for a winter fair in Knodishall, with jugglers, strongmen, acrobats, and men with dancing bears performing for the crowd. Primitive entertainment of a sort also came from 'Old Monty', the blind organ grinder, who lived with his wife and a gaggle of children of different sizes, half a dozen of his own and several 'taken in'. Monty would drag his machine around the district helped and guided by one of the children, who took this duty in turns. In his later years the children were made redundant when a benefactor provided him with a donkey to pull the barrel organ. The donkey, eventually learning the various circuits by heart, would set off with Monty in the morning and deliver him home again in the evening.

Newer technology arrived in Leiston in 1910 with Tommy Cottrell and 'Cottrell's Dramatic Picture Company' which was a bioscope show that projected photographic images inside a makeshift structure of wood and canvas that could be erected on any available open ground. This drew large audiences and the popularity eventually suggested to one or two men in the senior management of Garrett's that investment in a modern, purpose-built cinema might be a good thing, not just from an accounting point of view but from a paternal one, in that the workforce would be provided with an alternative to drinking in the growing town's many public houses. What Tommy Cottrell thought of the idea is unrecorded. A small paddock in a prime High Street location was purchased from Catlings, the adjacent butchers, and where grazing sheep and bullocks had awaited the knife, a cinema was built capable of seating an audience of 600 divided into three classes. In the spring of 1914, the doors of the Leiston Picture House opened to an excited public. Its success was to parallel that of another Leiston business which, located on the other side of the road opposite the cinema, was to become equally integral to the town's future social life.

Frank Maroelli had come to Leiston from Italy some twenty years earlier, attracted by the presence of a sizeable industrial workforce and the absence of any competition in his chosen profession of selling hot roast potatoes and chestnuts from a hand-pulled mobile brazier. Hard work, thrift and a good value product had enabled his progression first to a mobile fish and chip wagon towed by a horse, and then to permanent premises directly opposite the new cinema. Having become a man of substance, Frank then felt sufficiently confident to take enough time off to revisit Italy to search, successfully, for a wife. On their return to Leiston she worked beside him at the fryer to provide one of the essentials to what became established as the classic night out for most of the next century. A spare shilling in a workman's pocket would cover a cheap sixpenny seat at the cimema, a 'tuppenny and one' at Maroelli's (two pennies' worth of fish and a penny's worth of chips), with thruppence left over for a glass of beer on the way home. Two shillings was enough for a date.

Excitement even greater than that caused by the opening of the cinema had occurred a year earlier when, on 13 March 1913, a fire began in the early hours at George's place of work, the thresher department, which backed onto the High Street. Not only was the building itself old and made almost entirely of wood, but it housed piles and racks of the timber components used in the assembly of the threshing machines. Soon flames were rising fifty feet into the night, threatening the whole works. Seeing their employment at risk, Garrett employees of all ranks turned out in their hundreds to join with the Works brigade and the volunteer brigade from Saxmundham in fighting the fire. The draughtsmen removed their drawings to places of safety, others dragged out such components as could be salvaged and Frank Garrett joined in wherever help was most needed. By daybreak the fire had been mastered. The cooperative 'team' response to the crisis greatly improved subsequent management-workforce relations which had dipped severely in the aftermath of the temporary lock-out that had sent George to sea the previous year. This was despite the fire having started on the exact anniversary of the sackings that had precipitated the lock-out, a fact that was felt by many too unlikely to be coincidence. The thresher department, temporarily relocated to the Works Hall, was back in production within a week and George's employment, and his courtship, continued unchecked, despite the outbreak of war in the summer of 1914.

The only immediate impact of the war on George's life was that he found himself building horse-drawn carts and wagons for the British Army rather than threshing machines for the farmers, while the main body of the works turned to building steam engines and power plants for military applications. The men of the Works so employed were exempt from army service but, nonetheless, over 200 Garrett men volunteered for overseas duty within the first months of war, including Frank Garrett who, as a colonel in the Territorials, now found himself pitched against the nation of his erstwhile mentors, the people for whom he had developed such respect during his time in Halberstadt.

The Leiston men comprised most of 'H' Company of the 4th Battalion of the Suffolk Regiment. Seventy of them were killed or badly wounded in their first significant actions at Givenchy and Neuve Chappelle during the horribly wet and freezing first winter of war. News of their loss fuelled a new rush of recruits in the town, men anxious to avenge friends and workmates. On the day of their departure for training camp this second wave of volunteers marched from the Works Hall to the railway station with much pomp and glory, in step to the clash of cymbals and thump of drums from the Works band. A horse and cart from Leiston Hall Farm followed on behind to bring back the band's equipment as most of its members were leaving on the train. Once the cheering crowd and the smoke and steam had drifted away it trundled back down the sudden, sad quiet of Station Road, its load of shiny, unmanned instruments ominously symbolic.

Early in 1915 Frank Garrett was invalided home from France and, having experienced at first hand both the scarcity of shells brought about by Britain's antiquated military supply system and the efficiency of German production, he set about redressing the situation by launching the Works into a program of shell manufacture. Twin problems were the absence of suitable lathes – which the firm would normally have obtained from the Germans – and of men, who were fighting them. The answers were to adapt the machines they already had by mounting them upside down so that the piles of swarf created in turning shells dropped clear by gravity, and to employ women. Both solutions worked well after teething problems were overcome, particularly in the case of the women, who could be as volatile as the product.

The mass production of shells involved long shifts of monotonous, repetitive work which were alien to the nature of Garrett's usual hand-crafted manufacturing skills and so were resisted by the remaining men. The women recruited to do it in their place were from a wide spectrum of backgrounds, from respectable wives and daughters pleased to help with the war effort, to foul-mouthed characters happy to supplement their wages by use of whatever natural assets they might have. For all of them, the relative independence of the employment, the wages it earnt them and its companionable aspects combined to engender an atmosphere of high spirits that could make it a daunting arena for those entrusted with its supervision. A lady forewoman appointed on account of her gender rather than her management skills, felt it necessary to flee from a shrieking mob on the shop floor to the station opposite where, for protection, she locked herself in the stationmaster's office. Garrett's solution was to employ as supervisors a hardman, called Beswick, sufficiently robust to handle any verbal or even physical onslaught, and an ex-nurse who had been sacked for being drunk at work. These two between them were left by the Garrett management to get on with it and succeeded in moulding the ladies in their charge into a united and highly motivated team producing 7,000 heavy calibre shells every week.

By the middle of 1915 any fit young man of twenty in civilian clothes, whether employed in the making of army carts or not, was beginning to feel self-conscious on noticing pointed looks, real or imagined, from passers-by. The fear of somewhere encountering a deliberately positioned white feather, the shaming symbol of cowardice, propelled many young men not enamoured of the idea of war to join up against their better judgement. George was ambivalent: his character leaned naturally toward the pacifist but, on the other hand, the war was already on, many of his workmates had left to join it and, after all, life in the wood-working shop could be dull. For better or worse, and much against his mother's wishes, he decided to join up.

After making enquiries in Leiston, George was eventually directed to Cambridge where he was enrolled in the 2nd/4th Battalion The

Queens (Royal West Surrey Regiment) which was serving as part of the 160th Infantry Brigade. It was not particularly good timing for, after only a brief period of training with the battalion, he found himself at Devonport in mid-July, embarking for Gallipoli. Evacuated to Egypt just before Christmas he was one of the lucky few to have survived the ill-fated expedition, but the horrors of daily slaughter, and the grim conditions inflicted by the November blizzards, had not left him untouched. Always a quiet and introverted soul, he had never been emotionally robust, and was now a nervous and physical wreck with bronchial pneumonia threatening to achieve from within what the Turks had daily attempted with shells and bullets from without.

Through 1916, as the massacres of young men on the battlefields of France reached an unimaginable intensity, George struggled on under the beneficial influence of the Egyptian climate, but his spirit and his health had been broken. As the battalion prepared to mobilise against the Turks in Gaza he was invalided home, arriving at Mill House in February 1917 to find his father employed as a foundryman at the Works and Laura and Florrie gone from Highbury.

With the upheavals of war having left The Cupola empty and awaiting sale, Laura had thought better of her earlier decision and had returned to Mathew and her former employer in Wivenhoe. Florrie, seeing and seizing an opportunity for independence, had declined to go with her, preferring to wait for George in Leiston. Far too timid and fragile to consider joining the gangs on Garrett's shell lines, she found work as a chambermaid at Aldringham House, lodging at a terraced house in Central Road.

February turned cold enough to freeze Thorpeness Meare which Ogilvie opened to skaters, charging a shilling a day, soldiers and children half-price. Despite the icy weather George recovered his health sufficiently to rejoin the woodworking department at Garrett's where he was directed, not to make more horse-drawn carts for the Army, but to help assemble the wooden components of the latest war-machine – the FE2B aircraft which had been designed for the new Air Ministry with manufacture partially contracted to Garrett's.

Attention was focused on this new airborne aspect of warfare in the early hours of Sunday 17 June 1917 when Zeppelin L48, en route to bomb London, suffered engine trouble and a frozen compass over the coast at Orford and strayed northward towards Saxmundham after jettisoning its bombs near Ipswich. The giant airship, 650 feet long and weighing nearly thirty tons, was attacked by aircraft from Goldhanger in Essex and an FE2B from the experimental airfield on Orford Ness. On taking gunfire from Sergeant Ashby, the gunner in the latter plane, reputedly still wearing his pyjamas, it exploded in flame and fell into a field at Holly Tree Farm two miles north of Leiston, killing all but two of the nineteen crewmen. Most of the dead were found lying in a straight line, indicating that they must have jumped from the gondola of the blazing craft one after the other, perhaps hoping they were over the sea. Being a Sunday, the towering heap of twisted metal wreckage became a magnet for most of the local population for the rest of the day and, despite the presence of some soldiers detailed to guard the site, a considerable portion of it disappeared to be recycled into thousands of Zeppelin-shaped brooches. George, always good with his hands, made one for Florrie.

The courtship was developing well, perhaps more so than anticipated, as by the late autumn Florrie's slight frame could not conceal her pregnancy. The marriage took place on 5 February 1918 at St Margaret's Church in Leiston. The photographer captured the wedding party seated on a line of chairs beside a wall in the vegetable garden of Florrie's Central Road lodgings, shined shoes incongruous in the winter debris of a potato plot. The expressions are of people unaccustomed to formality but determined to acknowledge cause for happiness in a time of hardship. Charlie's curled moustache makes him seem to be smiling, though behind it he is serious. The calm confidence of his handsome wife Alice, then forty-five, could be mistaken for *hauteur*. Bride and groom look self-contained, in love. They moved into the front part of Mill House, using the bedroom kept for Harry Lucas, where, on 22 April, a son was born and named Jack.

Florrie's brief summer of independence had flowered but now withered under the steely rule of her mother-in-law. She was instructed in matters of laundry, household management, cookery, baby care, and husband care. And she was frequently inspected. On Monday wash-days Alice would run a critical eye over the laundry, lifting a corner of the sheets Florrie pegged out over the cobbled yard by the pump. The contents of cupboards and drawers were examined, and a finger run over the mantelpiece for dust: in *her* house things were to be done properly. Nor could the timid, soft-spoken Florrie expect any support in defence of privacy from her gentle husband, whose only hope of finding the confidence to confront his mother had been blown away with his nerves in the trenches of Gallipoli.

In November the Armistice was announced. At Sizewell Hall the cook, in a frenzy of elation, baked tray upon tray of sponge 'Armistice buns', throwing them madly about to children, staff and employers alike. At Garrett's munitions work ceased and, with war work no longer a necessity, George left the authoritarian environment he so disliked to become a journeyman carpenter. Maternal authority was not as easily avoided but George found quiet refuge in a private plan undertaken in the largest of the brick and tile sheds across the yard from Mill House.

The plan was inspired by the gypsies who came to camp on the Common at Knodishall each summer. Dark-skinned, black-haired and wild-eyed, they sat in smoky circles in front of tarred canvas tents, or perched on the steps of ornate, brightly-painted wooden caravans with protruding stove-pipes. Their shaggy piebald ponies were kept hobbled close by, competing with the rabbits for the grass that grew between the gorse bushes. They hawked handmade basketware and clothes-pegs from door to door, were regarded with deep suspicion and were blamed, rightly and wrongly, for the theft of anything that went missing. Their ragged offspring struck fear and wonder into the village children by scampering bare-footed across the prickly gorse and never attending school. Parents – themselves discomfited by primal fears stirred by the presence of these wild outsiders – perpetuated the fear and mystery with bedtime stories of kidnap and disappearance. But George envied them their freedom. Unable to escape the frustrating disciplines of his mother, he decided to build the means whereby he could if it really came to it. In the big shed he began, in periods of winter lay-off, to build a gypsy caravan.

The experience he had gained from making utilitarian army wagons at Garrett's was now employed in the creation of a thing of beauty. A little balustraded balcony enclosed a miniature red-painted door that shut with a smooth click. A blacked stove-pipe extended above the curved roof and Florrie stitched cushions for the cosy interior. During the winter evenings, behind the closed doors of the shed, the light of an oil-lamp reflected from its varnished paintwork as George worked making small improvements or adjustments, or simply stood gazing, running his hands over the smooth joints of the woodwork. He confided in Florrie that should Alice's dominating behaviour ever become unbearable they would find a pony and, with little Jack, take to the open road, free as the gypsies. Alice declared the caravan an outrageous waste but its mute threat may have helped keep her tyranny within bounds, for it only once left the big shed, for a weekend at Sizewell beach. More likely it was the understandable triumph of security over dreams that kept it there. But for George the solid existence of a means of flight away from his mother was more than just an insurance – it was a life-raft for his sanity.

Hard Times

In August 1920 Florrie gave birth to a daughter, Hilda, during a period when the men of Mill House were fully employed. George was enjoying a sustained run of work including employment on the construction of 'The House in the Clouds' at Thorpeness, an impressive Ogilvie eccentricity which disguised the resort's water tower as a house. Charlie remained at Garrett's foundry and Clifford was still on the land, but courting. Such relative security was not to last.

By the time Hilda was walking there were signs of the economic trouble ahead. The Bolshevik Revolution had written off a vast sum owed to Garrett's, Russia having been a major pre-war market for the firm. American exports were taking an increasing share of other traditional Garrett markets and the influence of Stephen Garrett, killed at Neuve Chappelle, was missed.

Before his death Stephen, Frank Garrett's third son, had argued the case for investigating the production of machinery based on the internal combustion engine. Now, in his absence, father and brothers persevered with steam, their concession to modernity being the production of some electrically-powered refuse carts for Glasgow Corporation. The outcome was inevitable. The miners' strike of 1926, and the subsequent absence of secure coal supplies, destroyed any remaining hope for sales of steam-powered equipment; electric vehicles proved not the way forward, and Charlie was laid off from the foundry. In the general economic decline local authority house-building programs halted and soon George was also out of work. The two men joined Clifford on Billy Smith's field gang of agricultural labourers, hand-pulling the sugar beet farmers had begun growing for the new Anglo-Dutch sugar factory in Ipswich.

At Mill House, as elsewhere, the situation was dire through the winter of 1926. Lacing up boots and pulling on coats for the cold, wet darkness outside was not the precedent to the heat of the foundry or the relative shelter of a building site, but to ten hours of back-aching work hunched in the freezing mud of the open beet fields. Raked by snow and sleet showers, with only a damp coat and a sack tied around the waist for protection, it was miserable employment, and for a pittance. Charlie at fifty-seven was getting too old for this sort of thing and planned a way out.

He had always grown more vegetables than the household could use, Alice selling the surplus from a glazed lean-to that extended into the yard on the north side of Mill House. Now, Charlie reasoned, father and two sons together could surely find a derelict cart and some sort of pony that, given George's wagon-building skills and a few carrots for horse-feed, they could turn into a delivery vehicle as the basis for developing a vegetable round.

An old four-wheel cart with no floor and missing wheel-spokes was obtained from Leiston Hall Farm and dragged home by the three men. George repaired it with the help of 'Chips' Woolnough, the carpenter from the forge located next door to Mill House, a business that also incorporated engineers, wheelwrights and undertakers. When each wooden wheel was ready with newly-shaved spokes tightly slotted in, it was laid flat on a circular slab of concrete on the Common opposite. Then, with heavy long-handled grips, the blacksmith and Chips would lift from the coke of the forge the glowing hoop of the iron wheel-rim and, carrying it quickly but cautiously between them, drop it over the wheel. A few bangs from a lump hammer to get the positioning just right and then steam would rise hissing and spluttering as George dowsed the iron with buckets of water, shrinking it tightly onto the timber, squeezing the spokes solidly home.

Charlie took to his spade to begin enlarging the vegetable garden and early in March started setting increased quantities of broad beans, peas, shallots and parsnips. An old pony, Maisie, was acquired at more than a fair price from Mr Becher at Bull's Hall Farm and the enterprise was ready to be launched. There was though, lurking unspoken, a possible problem with one of its proprietors. Clifford had quietly married the girl he had been seeing and the pair were now renting one of a pair of flint-walled cottages that stood on the corner of the Common a hundred yards or so from Mill House. The problem was that Clifford's emotional maturity was not altogether what it might have been. He did what he was told, in the fields or helping Charlie, but not being quite in tune socially, he was potentially a loose cannon. Alice, sensing the danger but saying nothing, worried about him and, having no faith at all in the capabilities of his wife Dorothy, insisted that Clifford take his every meal, including breakfast, at Mill House while Dorothy sat abandoned with their first infant son at home in Stone Cottages. It was not a healthy arrangement.

Out on the road with Maisie, the new vegetable round started reasonably well as Charlie knew so many of the working people of Leiston and the surrounding villages. His genial character and the fact that he asked only low prices was a great help but, given the worsening economic situation and an increasing number of lay-offs, an ever larger proportion of his customers made do with a carrot and an Oxo cube. Charlie surmised the answer to the problem lay in the enclave of Thorpeness where the rich continued to frolic each summer, seemingly unaffected by the poverty of the hinterland. So one July morning he and Clifford loaded the cart with a nice fresh display, harnessed Maisie and took the road through Aldringham towards the coast.

By mid-morning they were doing brisk business with the cooks and housekeepers of the summer lets and had covered no more than half the village when the striding, gaunt figure of Stuart Ogilvie appeared, having been tipped off to their presence by Graeme Kemp. Rapping the wheels of the cart with the swagger stick he kept under his arm Ogilvie roared at the two men 'How dare you indeed?! Hawking your bloody vegetables as if this was Battersea! Get off my land at once!' With that he gave poor Maisie, whose ears were already laid flat, a bad-tempered thwack on her rump with the stick.

Ogilvie, not without financial difficulties of his own incurred in the creation and promotion of Thorpeness during a period of recession, was anxious to preserve the refined tone of the resort come what may. Tradesmen were not to litter the avenues and no vulgar commercialisation was to be tolerated. A particular *bete-noire* was the increasing number of day-trip visitors, some of whom had the gall to actually picnic on the new golf course. In order to divert them Ogilvie persuaded the Leiston town council to take over the running of Sizewell beach to the north as an alternative destination for charabancs loaded with the *hoi-polloi* and also requested the Great Eastern Railway to stop advertising Thorpeness for seaside trips(as he had originally asked them to). A retired shepherd, Mr Chilvers, was appointed at £1 a week to undertake a golf course patrol to repel picnickers. Such attitudes, given the times and the project Ogilvie was struggling to execute, are understandable, but did nothing to modify the local view that Thorpeness was for toffs living in a world apart: an opinion supported by a communist party columnist in the *Leiston Observer* who ranted of Ogilvie 'there he sits, dazed with rich food!'

Dazed or not, Stuart Ogilvie died in March 1932, three weeks after a notice was posted on the main gates of the Works on 15 February announcing immediate closure. Three-quarters of the town's workforce was thus out of work. A desperate aura of helplessness gripped the population which had grown around its single large employer. The helplessness was increased by not knowing which way to turn to put food on the plate, for Leiston was uniquely isolated, an industrial town marooned amidst farms and estates that were themselves collapsing. Land was being sold off for as little as £3 an acre, if a buyer could be found, or lay derelict behind the untrimmed hedges spreading across the headlands.

Struggling to survive themselves, farmers exploited the unemployed, driving down piecework rates as they turned away the gangs of men asking for work in the fields: downcast men, who returned to damp, cramped houses without electricity, piped water or indoor sanitation. Water came from a well or from a brick-built rainwater tank, and was poured through muslin 'to get rid of the wigglies'. Sanitation was a pail or an earth closet, often perilously close to the well. In the early hours of the morning 'Moody' Bloomfield's horse and tanker-cart collected the pails of night soil produced over the previous twenty-four hours and tipped the amassed waste into 'Moody's Hole', located on an unfrequented part of the Common. This was a place of legendary horror amongst the village children. Jimmy Atkins' Alsatian dog, investigating a scent, once fell into it but survived. Moody, so named for his reticence, was late in collecting his pay from the council offices in Leiston one morning. 'Sorry' he managed 'but my wife was taken queer in the night.' Madge Fish, the clerk, in handing over the money said 'Well I do hope she's soon better Mr Bloomfield.' 'She on't be' said Moody, 'she died.'

Such seeming indifference may have been extreme, but apathy and resignation to a harsh and unfair life were deeply entrenched in the ordinary people who felt powerless to alter their fate. With morbid acceptance they watched youthful vigour spend itself until exhausted in the endless, unchanging struggle to simply get by. Those whose pride allowed it, or were forced by desperation, could apply for the meagre public assistance available to the truly destitute. It was never given until an inspector had conducted a means test, visiting the applicant's home to ensure that nothing saleable remained and that no possibility of employment existed. In Leiston Doris Wright, an ageing widow, took in washing for a few pence. On seeing the approach of a particularly officious inspector called Castleton she hurriedly dragged it from the line and threw it over the back fence onto the railway, but too late: Castleton had noticed and assistance was refused. Private charity could also be difficult to secure. Ogilvie's first wife Helen had given £52 per annum for the needy of Leiston, to be divided into eight half-crowns each week. There had never been a shortage of applicants; the problem was always the discrimination required to select the neediest. True charity sometimes came from humbler, unexpected sources.

Frank Maroelli had died, exhausted, not long after opening the fish and chip shop opposite the Picture House. His widow had little English and, finding it too difficult to continue, sold to another Italian, Peter Testoni. Leiston had liked Maroelli and welcomed the Italian following in his footsteps, a man of warmth, humanity and humour. These qualities, together with his general helpfulness, soon endeared Testoni to the town. But it was through the desperate years of the Depression that he established legendary goodwill by discreetly supplying fish suppers free to those whom local intelligence indicated needed them most. Testoni's support of the working man could not have been more straightforward or more practical. Help from their other Leiston champion was more theoretical.

The progressive educationalist A.S. Neill had founded his first school based on self-determination and free-thinking in Lyme Regis, but in 1927 he removed to Leiston, buying Richard Garrett's old house and re-naming it 'Summerhill'. Inevitably the people of a Victorian engineering town ruled by a factory hooter regarded it with detached amusement, quickly providing its alternative name of 'the do-as-you-like' school. Baker Peter Westbrook was pleased enough to produce a bespoke Summerhill loaf to a recipe provided by the Neills, which became quite popular but, as well as a new bread, Summerhill brought to the town a new voice, that of Paxton Chadwick.

Chadwick was a Manchester designer and artist, now the Summerhill art teacher and secretary to Neill. He was also a political activist and anti-fascist who, on discovering the plight of the town's unemployed, joined with other intellectual radicals at Summerhill to form local branches of the Communist Party and the National Unemployed Workers Movement. This group arranged a reception in Leiston for a contingent of the national Hunger March of 1934 when, as a consequence, over 1,000 people met in the Post Office Square: a demonstration of radical socialism that the people of the town could hardly have imagined had they not seen it. Chadwick continued his activism with the launch of a news-sheet *The Leiston Leader* which was a mouthpiece for Communist Party propaganda and the most extreme manifestation of the left-wing movement that developed in Leiston because of the presence of Garrett's, but despite the disinterest of most of its workforce. In terms of practical daily help Chadwick and his colleagues did their best, but could achieve little in the face of the worsening recession and a traditionally reactionary management at what was left of Garrett's.

Through all this hardship and privation the children played on, unsuspecting that life could offer more than a diet of bread and dripping and hand-me-down clothes mended and mended again. Their playground was the countryside around them and their pursuits traditional: dodging gamekeepers while collecting blackberries, mushrooms and birds' eggs; fishing in the farm ponds; swimming in the sea and diving for pennies thrown into the Minsmere River from the Tuppenny Arch bridge at Eastbridge.

As young children given 1*d* each by Florrie on a Saturday, Jack and Hilda would race each other across the Common to the cottage beside Charlie's Pond where old Mrs Smith sat in the gloom of a tiny lean-to, sometimes lit by a single candle, with a few jars of boiled sweets and a box of sherbet dabs. With an ounce of aniseed balls weighed into a twist of paper they would run to the bakers by the footbridge to lean against its gable wall and, sucking happily, warm their hands on the bolts that held the bread ovens in place on the other side.

William Goodwin's son Eric was one of their close friends. Whether because of further impertinence from his daughter Ruby, or simply due to hard times on the Ogilvie farms, William had left Ogilvie's employment for a job with the Weary sisters who had taken over Leiston Hall Farm in 1916. The family, which eventually included eleven children, moved to a thatch and flint tied cottage in Knodishall. This occupancy was cut short when William incurred the displeasure of the Weary's foreman by being favoured by the sisters to repair some machinery within the shelter and relative warmth of one of the farm sheds. The jealous foreman thought this plum job should be his, and explained his feelings to William. After further explanation of their respective feelings William threw the foreman into an adjacent ditch. His next job was with a farmer called Thurkettle at Manor Farm, Knodishall which involved moving to the primitive Meadow Cottages that stood against the far corner of the Common, a convenient location from which Eric and his siblings could join with the gangs of village children for whom the Common was an adventure playground.

At fourteen and about to leave school, Jack had grown tall but seemed too thin and pale. A worried Florrie eventually persuaded George to take him to the doctor in Leiston who diagnosed nothing basically wrong but advised that the boy should work in the fresh air rather than at Garrett's. Not that there was much chance of that given the prevailing shut-down at the Works. Encouraged by Eric Goodwin's father, Jack approached Thurkettle and was given a job looking after the bullocks that were fattened each winter in the yards of Manor Farm. Jack had not been there long when his employer suffered a serious injury while ploughing in the orchard beside the farmhouse. A gust of wind caused the sudden flap of a sheet on the washing line which sent the horse bolting. In an ill-advised attempt to halt it Thurkettle was thrown aside into the path of the wildly bouncing steel plough share which was dragged over one of his legs, crippling him. Thereafter he relied increasingly on Jack as his stockman and, by the spring of 1935, entrusted him with driving the store bullocks to Aldeburgh for the summer grazing, a job which he had previously undertaken himself. On arriving at the coast the cattle were driven through the town and out onto the Lantern Marshes that lie between the banks of the spit that separates river from sea beyond the Martello Tower. Ironically, this arrangement was to deliver to Jack leg problems of his own.

In that year the Lantern Marshes doubled as a bombing range for aircraft from the experimental aerodrome on Orford Ness at their southern end. The occasional bullock or sheep paid the ultimate price for this research but in October a pilot, either unseeing or badly misjudging, dropped a small bomb of about twenty pounds fifteen yards or so away from Jack who was checking the stock preparatory to bringing them back to Knodishall. When it exploded a piece of shrapnel made a hole in Jack's thigh big enough to put his thumb into, which he did to stop the bleeding. After he had managed to limp to the airfield for help, a military doctor was flown out from Martlesham aerodrome near Ipswich to repair the wound. Jack was sent home with a man from Leiston employed on the airfield, after being told sternly not to get in the way again. He was also advised to take a few days off work, which seemed a little superfluous as he was barely able to walk. The incident was officially recorded in the log book and the military authorities, geared to paying compensation now and again for inadvertently blowing up livestock, eventually forwarded compensation to Jack amounting to £4. In view of the six weeks it took to recover normal use of the leg, this seemed little enough.

By the time he was able to walk and work again Jack had decided farming and fresh air was far too dangerous. Instead of cycling up to

Manor Farm each morning he went on to Saxmundham to catch the train to Ipswich where he found employment at the sugar factory during the winter 'campaign' of processing sugar beet delivered in from the farms. Had he not been as averse to autocratic hierarchies as was his father, he might have gone to Garrett's: the Works had re-opened and was once again taking men on.

After the 1932 closure the receiver had eventually sold Garrett's to Beyer Peacock, a Manchester firm whose chairman was the high-living septuagenarian, Sir Sam Fay, a man who was rumoured to have his eye more on a lady with a house in Aldeburgh than on profits at Garrett's. Whether this was true or not – ownership of a challenging business far from home would certainly have provided perfect cover for an illicit affair – Garrett's resurrection had begun. By 1935 the men who had lost their jobs three years before had been reemployed, with more required. In that year, the final launching of the *Queen Mary*, left abandoned on the stocks in 1932, and the celebration of George V's Jubilee seemed symbols of hope. A focus on domestic affairs during the next two years – a period that saw the death of the King, Edward VIII's abdication and George VI's coronation – continued to divert attention from menacing developments in Europe. In any event, for the many who could remember 'the war to end all wars', a war that had finished less than twenty years earlier, it was unconscionable that such death, destruction and economic ruin could ever be repeated. The fact that Garrett's revival was increasingly based on a return to munitions contracts seemed incompatible with the general mood. 'What do you want to be making those things for?' was a frequent question asked of those who worked on the shell lines.

Just before 11am on 11 November 1937, Suffolk Regiment veteran Peter Smyth placed on the war memorial in Post Office Square a poppy he had picked on his return visit to the battlefield of Neuve Chappelle where so many Leiston men had died. 'The Bull' sounded, heads were bowed and all fell quiet until the sad cadence of 'The Last Post' rose from the trumpet of bandsman and town barber Kenny Pike. The mood was sober and reflective but would have been even more so had those present realised that by the following spring Garrett's would be delivering 4,000 cases of shells and mortar bombs each week to the Arsenal at Woolwich.

Three bicycles would leave Mill House at 6am each morning during 1936: George, canvas lunch-bag over his shoulder, pedalling doggedly off towards some distant building site, and the teenagers Jack and Hilda pushing energetically along School Road towards Saxmundham. Charlie, now sixty-six, and Clifford would stay to tend the garden and work the vegetable round. Fourteen-year-old Eric would join Hilda and Jack near the red-brick Victorian schoolhouse that all of them had attended and, as Jack pressed on for the train, he and Hilda he would peel off downhill towards the Peets at Knodishall Hall Farm where Hilda was housemaid and Eric was 'back'us boy'. It was Hilda's job to help Mrs Peet make the beds, sweep, boil laundry and churn butter while Eric would be lighting fires, fetching coal, cleaning boots, pumping water up into the roof tank and, towards Christmas, helping Mr Peet pluck the turkeys.

There were not many to pluck in 1937 as the turkey cock Mr Peet had retained for breeding proved to be impotent, an unhappy fact only discovered after weeks of futile incubation of the eggs, and too late in the year for a replacement cock to be of much use. The violent revenge exacted on the unlucky bird by Mr Peet's hob-nailed boots resulted in its premature death and a bad memory that stayed with Hilda for the rest of her life. It may have helped instil her lifelong compassion for the underdog, and certainly encouraged her to seek new employment in the new year.

Eric – whose father was still with Thurkettle just across the road at the Manor Farm – had had enough of boots and turkeys too and moved to a job at Leiston Hall Farm with the Weary sisters. Evidently they did not hold against the boy his father's earlier rough treatment of their foreman. In the spring Hilda found work in Thorpeness as housemaid and nanny to the two young sons of Mrs Grace Agate. The Agates lived at a different social level from her previous employers, maintaining a second residence in London and a lifestyle free of the more earthy chores associated with a farm. This more sophisticated and sometimes cosmopolitan household suited Hilda's confident, curious nature and the employment progressed well. The Thorpeness house itself stood next to The Meare on Lakeside Avenue, very close to 'The Ness House' where the following year, in August 1939, Lady Tufnell arrived for a holiday accompanied by her maid, Anne Jordan.

Ed

On Long Island Edwin Rosenthal was growing up in a very different environment. His mother *employed* maids and although Sig's business had its ups and downs the overall tenor of life was well-to-do. When underwear sales went down Alpha would assist the family budget by taking commissions for portraits. When they went up she would ease off, much to the relief of Sig who regarded his wife painting commercially as a slight to his abilities as a businessman.

Ed began high school at the Woodmere Academy in 1928 and was soon achieving high marks as well as selection for various school sport teams. While older brother Larry might have been more focused on career success as a lawyer, and younger brother Bob was less focused generally, it was Ed's creative and enquiring mind that propelled him to graduate top of his year in 1932. His inclination to seize life with all its myriad and romantic possibilities could put him at odds with his father who favoured the single-minded slog approach that had brought *him* his success and was now exemplified by brother Larry.

With an outstanding high school record behind him, Ed had no difficulty in entering Yale for his freshman college year but had hardly settled in when a football injury to his back and suspected tuberculosis caused his doctor to advise him a to the dry heat of somewhere like Arizona. Ed, who had thought of the West as his destiny ever since grandmother Meema had filled his childhood dreams with stories of the old frontier, jumped at the chance and enrolled at the University of Arizona in Tucson. Blue skies and the bright white-washed Spanish colonial architecture appeared to offer an escape to his mother's world of open spaces and relaxed living, but it was not without a downside. At home in the Jewish-dominated suburbs of Woodmere, Ed had failed to foresee that 'out West' the larger proportion of, in his words, 'red-neck, blue-shirt and fascist-minded people' would see him as a 'New York Jew-boy'. It was a shock, particularly, as in line with Sig's abandonment of his old world heritage, Ed had never even been to a synagogue, much less regarded himself as a Jew.

Another shock had occurred when Ed overheard his father's comment to his mother as, waiting to leave on the first leg of the journey to Tucson, he waved from the open window of the train standing at Woodmere station. Apparently with little faith in Ed's survival prospects, Sig turned away from the departing train and said rather too loudly to Alpha that 'the next time we see that boy he'll be in a box.' The detached coolness of the remark probably stemmed from Sig's own exile in 1896, but nonetheless it planted a seed of insecurity deep in Ed's psyche.

The University of Arizona was not in the same league as Yale but there was the weather and a reasonable English department with a university newspaper to serve Ed's growing commitment to journalism. This ambition, perhaps first fired by Meema's ability to weave a good story, had been clinched when Ed, seeking career advice, called on senior *New York Times* reporter, Joe Shaplen, at his apartment in Greenwich Village. At 11am Joe was just out of bed, reading the morning's papers preparatory to a 2.30pm start at the news desk. That appealed to Ed, always an amateur *bon viveur*, in favourable contrast to the awful 6am reveilles that his father had observed throughout a lifetime of commuting into New York City on the Long Island Railroad. Brother Bob joined Ed at the university in 1934 but by then Ed, encouraged by his English tutor, had realised that if he was serious about becoming a newspaperman he would need to transfer his final year to a university with a nationally recognised school of journalism. One of the acknowledged best was at the University of Wisconsin in Madison.

Journalist or not, Ed was certainly a good correspondent, typing letters home regularly, often weekly, throughout the first decade after his departure from home. Giving news of his day-to-day life interspersed with opinions on national and international issues, these letters are addressed to 'the folks' but it is clear that Ed writes first for his adored mother, then for his father, and then for his younger brother – Larry is seldom mentioned. The sentences pulsate with the excitement of youth, with descriptions of new places and people, with anticipation of future adventures. They gasp with appreciation of the sun-washed grandeur of Arizona's desert mountains and of the vast, violet south-western sunsets. Later, amid the daily-changing, almost fluorescent autumn colour of Madison's northern campus, with its vistas across the whitecaps of the lake to the brown plough-lands, Ed is overwhelmed, not just by the aesthetics but by the intellectual excitement of his new independence. In *faux bierkellers* he argues politics and literature as classical music drifts from the music studios, escaping through windows left open to the warm autumn air adrift with scarlet leaves, wood-smoke and possibilities.

Graduating in the spring of 1936 at the height of the Depression with newspapers closing weekly, Ed persevered with chasing contacts and eventually, on 7 August, was able to telegraph home the exciting news that he had been taken on for a trial period as a cub reporter on *The Buffalo Times* in upstate New York at $18 a week. The trial was successful and his brief was expanded to cover sports news, radio reviews and obituaries. He had two complaints: the first that there were too few column inches available for local news as the paper, like most, was preoccupied with Edward VIII's abdication for the love of the American, Wallace Simpson. He couldn't resist relaying home, in case they hadn't heard it, the apocryphal story of Mr Simpson's divorce court comment when, paraphrasing the American Revolutionary War hero Nathan Hale, he was reported to have said 'My only regret is that I have but one wife to lay down for my King.'

The second problem was less transitory: Buffalo lies close to Niagara Falls on the Canadian border and winters are extreme. For someone appreciative of physical comforts the vicious snow storms and months of sub-zero temperatures compared unfavourably with the year-round outdoor life in Arizona, or even with Madison, given the absence of warming student conviviality. Halfway through his second winter Ed was overjoyed when his kindly chief editor found him a job on a sister paper *The Buffalo* in Houston, Texas. Soon Ed was swimming in Galveston Bay and taking adventurous trips down into Mexico.

Sometimes these could become too adventurous as when he was arbitrarily arrested by Mexican police conducting a fund-raising operation in the border town of Laredo. On his way back to the US after a late night in the cheap Mexican bars, Ed was dragged from the street to a police barracks where he was horrified to discover he was without his wallet and thus the $2 bribe necessary to secure his release. Consequently he spent the night in an un-plumbed cell with several incontinent drunks and *gringo*-hating criminals and, worse, faced the prospect of a ten-day stint on a road gang. Fortunately in the morning his drinking companion noticed his absence and arrived at the police station with the required $2.

It was during these trips into Mexico that Ed noted the corrupting influence of tourism. American visitors, he reported to the family, sought out American hotels, American food and American companions. So doing they insulated themselves from the indigenous people and their culture, refusing any experience that could modify their preconceived notions of either. He noticed how keen the Mexicans were to learn English so that they might offer themselves as guides to the tourists who were inevitably duped into paying ten or twelve times the normal rate for food and accommodation. For his own part, having only a junior reporter's wage, Ed travelled as cheaply as he could, camping or staying in primitive farmhouse guest-rooms. At one, the seventeen-year-old daughter of the hosts was struggling to read to her numerous younger siblings a Grimm's fairy tale in English. She asked Ed for help and so, cross-legged under the stars of a desert night, he slowly read and explained to a fire-lit circle of small faces why the sea is salty.

In Mexico City a mural by the famous Jose Oruzco had him stretching for superlatives. A fiery scene depicting war, sex, genocide, the destruction wrought by industrialisation and the general collapse of civilised society, it was an expression of revolutionary socialism, an 'art of the people'. Ed described it to his mother as one of the greatest things he had ever seen. It was an encouragement towards the left-wing thinking he was already developing at a time when communist sympathies had yet to be disillusioned. Such thoughts and travel would not have been undertaken by his brothers and were establishing Ed as the bohemian of the three.

Gradually life in Houston palled. The Texas seaboard was not the West: it was 'red-neck, cotton state, bible-belt' country and Ed began to realise his liberal thinking was making him uncomfortable in such a reactionary climate, however amenable the physical one might be. He borrowed $800 from his father, bought a new Plymouth coupe and headed west of the Pecos. He stopped when he got to San Francisco and found a job as sports editor on the city's evening newspaper, *The Call-Bulletin*.

Above 'that blue and windy Bay' Ed felt he had discovered his *El Dorado*; it seemed the west coast dreams Meema's bedtime stories had inspired twenty years earlier would be fulfilled in the city where she had spent her wedding night. San Francisco captured his heart. His responsibilities at the paper, his salary and his social life all accelerated. Competence at the job required close contact with the city's social and political hierarchies: letters home were now crammed with descriptions of parties, dinners and grand events. Interviews had to be conducted with the great and famous: poet and writer Carl Sandburg on his new Pulitzer Prize-winning biography of Lincoln; Hemingway on his newly-published *For Whom The Bell Tolls*. He was invited to become a member of the San Francisco Press Club, an august collection of oak panelling, leather armchairs and old men, the latter inclined to believe that, if one had not been in the city to report on the great earthquake and fire of 1906, one had missed the boat in the press world.

Nor was there any shortage of young women keen to be escorted to parties and happenings where Ed's press credentials provided the *passeporte* (at that time, well before their profession was undermined by sensationalist tabloids, newspapermen commanded a great deal more respect than would later be the case). Despatched to report on training progress at the San Francisco Giants' baseball camp in the hills east of the city, Ed took a young lady with him and together they explored the melancholy ruins of Jack London's burnt-out house, its collapsed stone walls and charred timbers being reclaimed by the forest of eucalyptus and redwood. With friends he explored the coast north of the Golden Gate bridge, spending idyllic days swimming in the clear, fast waters of the Russian River and sunbathing on the shingle bars dividing its shallows. In stimulating company, in turns laughing or earnest with discussion of the day's issues, he drank beer and ate barbecued chicken in small-town restaurants hidden amongst the hills that rise above the fog banks that linger over the cold vastness of the Pacific.

Grandmother Meema visited from Seattle in October 1939, prompting Ed to dedicate the weekend to driving her back to Placerville, the birthplace and hometown she had not seen since leaving on her wedding day fifty-one years previously. It was a great success: childhood friends were rediscovered, stories retold, and tears shed. At 61 Coloma Street, the wooden house her father had built in 1849 still stood, complete with the maple tree in the front yard that Meema had climbed as a child. Ed loved it as much as she did. He was like a man with a camera, aware that every new view might have the potential for a great shot: in his case, each new turn, every incident, could be a story. This constant possibility was to encourage an engagement with people across the whole spectrum of human experience, an attitude that would serve him well in the years ahead.

Writing to brother Bob who had returned to New York to help Sig run the family business – now suffering the effect of cheap imports from Puerto Rico – Ed told him not to be downcast by events in Europe. Rather, he advised, see them as mere brushstrokes on the great canvas of world history and exalt in being contemporary to them. Undoubtedly that was how Ed felt as he registered with his local military draft board, only to find himself classified 4F; in other words, rejected. For a fit young man who must have quietly enjoyed the realisation that he was living a life not too dissimilar from that of his contemporary hero Hemingway, rejection came as a shock. He inquired the reasons for the classification. No satisfactory answer was forthcoming and Ed, smelling a rat, proposed the theory that, as his boss at *The Call-Bulletin* did not want to lose him, and as the examining doctor was brother to the newspaper's publisher, there had been a conspiracy. Whether or not this was fanciful thinking, resignation to civilian life in San Francisco was not too uncomfortable to accommodate: at least until the Japanese attacked Pearl Harbour on 7 December 1941.

Suddenly the war was a lot closer. Flotillas of warships steamed to and fro under the Golden Gate. Military aircraft roared overhead. Market Street, the city's main thoroughfare, filled with uniformed troops. Girls began to take over men's jobs. Occasional blackouts were enforced. Submarines were reported lurking offshore.

Patriotism compelled Ed to again query his 4F status. At this, the secretary of the draft board discovered an error had been made: in fact his classification should have been 1A from the outset. Someone had accidentally ticked the wrong box. Ed had been fit for service for over a year whilst believing himself a physical wreck or else the victim of scheming employers! Leaving the secretary's office, he hurried to the nearest recruitment centre planning to enlist in the hope of being able to choose a branch of service appropriate to his skills, rather than leaving the decision to the draft board and probably ending up a foot soldier. It worked to a degree: his talents in the field of communications were noted and by the spring Ed was in uniform at an army camp in Reno, Nevada training as a Morse code operator for the Signal Corps. Sig was disgusted that his middle son had not applied for officer training like Larry.

War

By the summer of 1939 Hilda Thorpe was an attractive, self-pos-
sessed young woman with a reputation for irreverent high spirits.
In that year Hilda Spoore was a ten-year-old Knodishall school-
girl and recalls often seeing her older namesake pedalling to work
in Thorpeness. She remembers her as outgoing and friendly, always
neatly turned out and very clean. The last an unusual adjective maybe,
but one which betrays the primitive facilities for personal hygiene in
the cottages and houses of the village. More interesting than 'clean',
Hilda Spoore noticed she was often 'made up' with long blonde hair
set off by lipstick and powder. She also knew from the village grape-
vine that the vivacious Hilda Thorpe was fond of a laugh, a cigarette
and a drink. Thinking back she remembers her as both fascinating
and inspiring, flying past on the Aldringham Road with a friendly
wave and a puff of smoke.

It was inevitable that in Thorpeness that August Hilda Thorpe
and Anne Jordan would meet and recognise in each other the rebellious, fun-loving nature that would unite them in a lasting friendship.
Both women enjoyed flirting with Victor Kersey, the good-looking
delivery boy from the Thorpeness Stores. Joining forces in Mrs Agate's
or Lady Tufnell's kitchen when these employers were out, they would
use the telephone to place an order for perhaps nothing more than
a box of matches, knowing that within a few minutes Victor would
arrive at the back door on his high-handled delivery bicycle, ready
for risqué repartee. But Victor was only a diversion, a lad in his teens:
Anne was twenty-three and true love lay elsewhere.

Instructed by Florrie to invite her Irish friend home for tea, Hilda
brought Anne to Mill House one Sunday afternoon late in the month.
There, facing Bovril sandwiches and strong tea on the lace-clothed
table in the little sitting room off the kitchen, she sat beside Hilda's
brother Jack. The attraction was immediate and mutual. Later, in the
near dark, with no lights on their bicycles but a new light in her eyes,
Anne raced Hilda furiously back to Thorpeness. It proved to have
been the last weekend of peace. Within a month Jack had enlisted in

the Royal Navy and was training on the south coast. Anne was back in St Albans, shortly to be directed to war work at a factory making aircraft instrumentation. Hers would, of necessity, be a courtship by correspondence.

On the Suffolk coast, the same geography that had kept the area an isolated rural backwater far to the east of London now put it directly in the path of the expected German invasion. Its sparse population, terse of speech and suspicious of strangers, had been shaped and weathered by legacies of tradition rooted in the old England of Elizabeth. As Suffolk historian Alan Jobson put it, this was 'an inheritance to be handed on as the furnishings of the cottages and the implements of the field'. Change gained a foothold only slowly against the resistance of inertia. But in 1939 the imperatives of war imposed on this remote place all the sudden realities of twentieth-century warfare with neither time nor chance for dissent.

Thousands of troops trucked in to install and man coastal defences. Minefields were laid. Barriers of barbed wire and 'dragon's teeth' were erected along the shoreline. Long rows of concrete block 'tank traps' were set up to direct the armoured vehicles of the enemy into lines of fire from pillboxes and gun emplacements. Searchlight batteries were built to illuminate incoming bombers for the anti-aircraft gunners. The coast was declared a closed area for all but essential purposes and the woods and heaths of the hinterland filled with army camps and training areas. At Sudbourne, five miles south of Knodishall, the residents of the entire village with its surrounding farms were ordered to vacate their homes to facilitate the creation of a live firing range. The hamlet on the beach at Shingle Street was also evacuated and its buildings relegated to practice bombing targets.

At Garrett's all employable men, and increasingly women, worked double shifts to produce shell cases and naval gun mountings at a rate which soon outran the availability of guns to utilise them. Thereon an Admiralty inspector visited the Works and, finding himself impressed by the professional attitude and competence of management and workforce alike, awarded a contract for the manufacture of the guns themselves. It then struck the management

– all too aware of its exposed position on the eastern-most coast of Britain – that it would be a good idea to install, even, if necessary, at its own expense, six of these guns at strategic locations around Leiston to be manned by a special Works platoon of the Home Guard.

Formed in June 1940, this platoon was also provided with rifles and ammunition and trained every Sunday on Sizewell Common. Here, at times, the men were required to simulate a combat situation by running ten yards, throwing themselves to the ground, firing, getting up, running another ten yards and so on in proper military style. As it was deemed far too dangerous to use live ammunition for this exercise, five Christmas cracker-style bangers were taped to the barrel of each rifle with one being pulled each time it was necessary to signify a shot. The worth of this part-time training, and of the Leiston guns, looked set to be tested late in the evening of 7 September when Frank Andrews, the commander of the local Home Guard, received a message from his HQ stating 'Invasion expected tonight. Man all guns.' In great haste bicycles were mounted and battle positions taken up as excited, fearful eyes strained into the blackness searching for paratroopers or panzers. No one realised the message was, fortunately, a mistake.

In fact a successful, if limited, German invasion had already occurred during the first winter of the war if one believed 'Smoky' Joe, a salt-pickled ex-fisherman and proprietor of a primitive tar and tarpaulin teahut adjacent to the Sizewell-Leiston road. Famed for its eye-watering atmosphere, Smoky's enjoyed a brief period of prosperity with the influx of troops to the coast, until several cases of food poisoning resulted in its being placed out of bounds by the authorities. Some months after the event Smoky reported that he had regularly provided food, water and information to a submarine crew camped out in the woods near Sizewell. They explained away their strong German accents by claiming to be Dutch, but Smoky was sure they were picked up from the beach one night by a U-boat. It is possible that Smoky unwittingly inflicted some early casualties on enemy forces.

So likely was the expected invasion that a secret underground resistance network of men was trained and installed along the coastal strip with the objective of sabotaging supplies and communication behind the lines of the advancing invaders should they manage a successful landing. In Leiston seven Garrett employees were selected for this specialist training and supplied with a hidden subterranean dugout on Sizewell Common, its location, in theory at least, known only to them. It was all top-secret, serious stuff involving cyanide capsules for a hasty exit if captured.

As well as positioning the six guns and sponsoring a platoon of the Home Guard dedicated to their operation, Garrett's invested in substantial camouflage works, blackout provisions and air-raid shelters. In the event there was no orchestrated air attack on the Works, although significant production time was lost as the result of staff taking shelter following soundings of the air raid warning siren. As the siren was usually triggered by high-level bombers en route to London, the absence of a subsequent local attack soon saw initial alarm replaced by a nonchalant determination on the part of most people to keep calm and carry on. Those few of timid disposition conscientiously took shelter every time the siren went off.

In Knodishall this category included old Mrs Moore, whose family owned one of the two village shops, and her two elderly neighbours Mr and Mrs Felgate. Day or night, whenever the siren wailed, these three each picked up a prepared bag containing their most treasured items and trooped dutifully into a wooden shed that stood in the garden of the Felgates' terraced cottage. Here they would sit facing each other until the 'all-clear' sounded, presumably confident of not being buried alive should their houses be hit, and no doubt drawing comfort from being together. The shed was roofed with corrugated tin which suggested to Hilda and two friends Molly Felgate and Nancy Moore, granddaughters of the sheltering old folk, that the elders would be encouraged to believe their routine was not in vain if each girl lobbed two or three half-bricks onto the tin. Over the crash and clatter of the bricks Mrs Moore was heard to cry 'We're being bombed!' whereon poor Mrs

Felgate began trembling so violently her husband feared she would suffer a seizure.

Inevitably tragedy occasionally emphasised that a cavalier attitude to air-raid warnings could be fatal, particularly when lone German aircraft flew in from the sea seeking targets of opportunity. Two boys playing football on the Recreation Ground in Leiston ignored the school caretaker's shouted warning to take cover and were killed by a bomb intended for Garrett's. A third was buried alive but was dug out in time. On Waterloo Avenue Mr and Mrs Hicks were killed in the rubble of their sweetshop and, in Aldeburgh, the post office was demolished with the loss of eleven lives and twenty-nine injured when a Dornier suddenly appeared from low cloud to bomb and strafe the High Street. Nancy Moore recalls being out on her bicycle between Leiston and Knodishall when she heard a plane approaching from behind, following the road. As it roared low overhead it dipped one wing and she was horrified to see the black crosses of the Luftwaffe on its fuselage while the leather-helmeted pilot smiled and cheerily waved.

On the land 'the War Ag.' directed that maximum effort be employed to increase food supplies by converting rough grazings and heather sheep 'walks' to arable production. Huge gyro-tillers cleared scrub-infested fields and overgrown hedges preparatory to ploughing land which, in places, had lain neglected since the end of World War I. Employment either on the farms or at Garrett's was classed as a reserved occupation giving exemption from military service, but, as many men nonetheless volunteered, there was a general shortage of manpower. To help overcome the problem the Ministry of Labour was authorised to allocate work to all those capable of it, male and female. Many men having grown up through the dispiriting inter-war years of the Depression now found themselves facing the twin novelties of year-round employment and female workmates. Certainly the young women were not blind to the increased opportunities presented by war work and a coast full of troops, although scarce alcohol and the difficulty of going anywhere on a winter evening during the blackout were handicaps to a night out. Another temporary setback to wartime romance occurred when a girl was murdered by a soldier in a corn field at Aldringham. In an area where occasional incest and a tradition of smuggling had been the only notable crimes, murder was unimaginable. The soldier was convicted after grains of rye were discovered lodged in his battledress.

The downside to this increased tempo of rural life was that the country was on its knees as it waited for the expected German invasion during the summer of 1940. The increasing success of the U-boats in sending merchant ships to the bottom of the Atlantic resulted in severe shortages of all commodities, not least food and clothing. Rationing of essentials such as meat, butter, sugar, tea and cheese restricted purchases to a few ounces per person each week while 'exotic' items such as bananas and oranges were either una-vailable or were reserved for 'green' coupons for children under the age of five. Equally many household items such as pots or kettles could not be purchased as the war effort consumed all available steel and manufacturing capacity. Beer was in short supply and even when a pub found itself in receipt of a delivery there were often insuf-ficient pint glasses to serve the sudden rush of customers demanding it. Locals resolved this problem by taking a two-pound jam jar with them when going out for a drink. Clothing was patched and re-patched, sheets were cut and re-sewn 'sides to middles' and nothing was thrown away: for many women brought up in the Depression and living through the war this was a legacy that would stay with them for life. Rural areas like Knodishall were at some advantage in being close to the source of food production, although bureaucratic control was everywhere and it was unwise to be seen, either from the official or neighbourly viewpoint, to be advantaging oneself. 'Don't you know there's a war on?' was a common disapproving question, as Russell Ling knew well.

Russell lived in Valley Road, Leiston and worked for farmer David Easy, a tenant of Ogilvie farms at Leiston and Knodishall. One dark Friday night late in 1940 Easy knocked on his employee's door to ask him to come over to Knodishall to look at a sick pig: Easy relied on Russell as an excellent stockman. By the light of an oil lamp and a torch the two men found the pig stuck fast underneath a heavy timber cattle manger, squealing horribly as its fellows set about it. Russell saw immediately its back was broken and declared 'that on't nivva be na good'. Easy, realising the truth of this, offered the pig to Russell who accepted it gladly and having his wages in his pocket, it being a Friday, offered to pay for it. 'No, no' said Easy 'I'll just have a piece if you get on alright with it.'

The partially paralysed pig, now semi-conscious, was loaded into Easy's van and driven to Leiston where, under cover of darkness, Russell loaded it into a wheelbarrow, covered it with some sacks and pushed it up his long garden path straight into his back kitchen-cum-scullery. This was all highly improper, as the movement, slaughter and sale of pigs was subject to a system of strict control by permit. Knowing there were busy-body neighbours who might well spill the beans, Russell obscured the kitchen windows with a variety of old coats and jerkins as he got a fire going under the copper ready to process the pig, which at this stage was still alive. Russell owned a shotgun but, realising a shot in the night might attract unwanted attention, he silently despatched the unfortunate pig with a blow between the eyes from a heavy coal hammer.

Bleeding, eviscerating, scalding, de-bristling and removal of the pig's toenails (to make the 'trotters' look attractive) was all going well, and Russell was covered in gore and sweating heavily in the small steamy kitchen, when suddenly there was a knock at the door and a call 'Mr Ling?' Cursing under his breath Russell shouted back loudly 'Yes, can I help you?' and was mortified to hear the response: 'Police! We've got a licence here with it written on when you can move your pig.' This related to another pig altogether, a legal one, which Russell was fattening on his allotment. Russell, whilst disclaiming any religious inclination at all, admits that in moments of crisis something approaching divine inspiration has often come to his rescue. He called back 'thank ya but would ya mind goin' ter tha front door cos ah'm hevin' a bath. Me wife is in the front room

– she'll see to it.' Happily Russell realised his claim would be corroborated by the absence of the tin bath from its hook on the outside wall beside the back door, the oval of lighter brickwork plain for the police to see in their torchlight. It was, of course, the pig that was in the bath.

The younger of the two policemen – who was a trainee up from somewhere near London – turned to the sergeant, a Leiston man, and asked 'Did you hear what he said?' 'Yes' answered the sergeant 'most of these people don't have any sort of bathroom – just the old tin bath.'

The trainee's surprise was because drainage from Russell's kitchen floor and sink exited through a small hole in the wall to an open gully which then crossed the path to a grate-covered soakaway drain. Unknown to Russell, gulley and grate had become blocked with leaves blown from the roof of the house and a noxious mix of blood and guts was now spilling down the path and eddying around the shiny black shoes of the policemen. 'Do they bath very often?' said the youngster aghast, shining his torch down at the bits of dirty straw, huge toe-nails and small pieces of innards at his feet. The sergeant, who knew full well what Russell was up to, replied 'Well if he's having a bath we don't want to disturb him because he can surely do with it!'

Through the first winter of war Hilda continued to work for the Agates in Thorpeness although, having registered for war work, she expected at any moment to receive direction from the Ministry of Labour to join the shell lines at Garrett's. Occasionally she accompanied Mrs Agate and the boys to their London house and it was during one such absence from Thorpeness that a Requisitioning Officer noted the Agates' Lakeside Avenue house as being empty. After Hilda had returned, leaving the Agates in London, she opened the door to this officer one morning to be informed that the house was required for military use and would be occupied more or less immediately. Seeing no problem with this – after all, invasion was imminent – she provided such information as was requested and stayed on to welcome in the troops over the next few days, no doubt helping them feel at home with cups of tea and quite probably the contents of the sideboard. Unfortunately it seems no one reported these developments to Mrs Agate who returned home a week later to find the house with its fine period furniture fully occupied by the Army. Horrified, she sacked Hilda on the spot, although domestic services were now largely irrelevant in any case.

On hearing of this calamity, Annie quickly came to her friend's rescue by recommending Hilda for a post with an aristocratic friend of Lady Tufnell's in St Albans. Annie's reputation meant that her judgement was respected and within the week a letter arrived at Mill House with an offer of employment. Hilda replied with a refusal and then wrote to Anne explaining that grateful though she was, the prospect of continued domestic service was too hard to bear: she just did not want to serve at table ever again. Perhaps if Anne could find her work in a shop or a factory she would look for lodgings in St Albans and they could be together again. The idea became a reality more quickly than they might have expected when the authorities directed Anne to join the workforce at the nearby E.A.C. factory, obliging her to leave her employment and accommodation with Lady Tufnell.

Still no call had come from Garrett's, so Hilda, wanting to do more than simply help Florrie at home, acted on information received from Anne and asked if she too might be employed at E.A.C. – Anne's sister Agnes had also left domestic service at the outbreak of war and was working as a conductor on the St Albans buses. The two Irishwomen had found accommodation at 130 Waverley Road in rooms rented from Mrs Izzard, a cook at the local services restaurant, and, on receiving consent to her request, Hilda set off on the train to join them. During the day, dressed in a pair of brown factory overalls, she checked the calibration of instruments destined for the cockpits of bomber aircraft: in the evenings the three girls set out on sorties of their own to the pubs and dance halls of the town. Yet increasingly it seemed as if Anne's heart was elsewhere as she continued an intense correspondence with Jack, now serving in the Far East.

Eric

On 10 March 1940, Eric Goodwin woke up to the morning of his eighteenth birthday with the main business of the day clear in his mind. Having arranged with the Wearys to take the day off work, he joined three friends of similar age to cycle to Saxmundham to catch an early train for Ipswich. Joshing and joking, partly with the high spirits of a day out but also to hide a little nervousness, the four young men strode out from Ipswich station towards the recruiting office, each determined to enlist as a Royal Marine. Only one was accepted. Medical tests revealing a hernia, poor eyesight and weak lungs eliminated the three friends, leaving burly, six-foot Eric the only successful candidate. Invited to sign up, he committed himself to twelve years service.

Initial training began within the week on the Channel coast when, at 4pm one afternoon, the train down from London discharged some 150 new recruits onto the platform at Deal station. A sergeant-major quick-marched them off to temporary barracks where he instructed them to stuff their pallias sleeping mats with straw and to 'make a bloody good job of it or you'll regret it!' Eric took the advice to heart and later that night found himself balancing facedown atop a near cylindrical mat, his arms clutched around it as if around an over-inflated sleeping partner. But within a day or two the straw had crushed down nicely and those who had been less enthusiastic in their stuffing found themselves uncomfortably intimate with the floor.

Eric was sent down to train on the Devon coast at Exmouth but within a few weeks the Dunkirk evacuation was underway and he was sent back to Kent. His platoon took up a position on the cliffs of South Foreland from where they watched for over a week as a desperate rag-tag procession of boats and ships struggled back from France harried by German aircraft. There was little they could do to help, being equipped with only a light Bren-gun on high-elevation mounts, intended to provide an adjacent searchlight battery with protection from air attack. Unfortunately the range and calibre of the gun was grossly inadequate for the task and a dangerous position was exacerbated by their inability to dig in, as the uncovering of fresh chalk on the cliffs would have pin-pointed their position beyond the ability of camouflage nets to disguise it.

Training completed, Eric was sent to Liverpool in the spring of 1941 to act as batman to a Marines officer on the way to join his ship at Capetown. They were to travel south on a Dutch-crewed tramper forming part of a convoy transporting military supplies to the British Army in Egypt and the Middle East. Weighing anchor in the late afternoon, the convoy lost two ships before rounding Anglesea, sunk by a U-boat lurking in the approach lanes of the Irish Sea. First light saw another four ships sunk as the convoy progressed slowly down St George's Channel. Then, with the Atlantic opening before it, and lacking adequate escort protection, the convoy scattered to provide less of a concentration of targets.

The Dutch skipper of Eric's vessel, having already had one command sunk from under him, decided on a bearing taking them west and south of the direct route to the Cape, hugging the coast of South America almost to the Falklands before swinging east. Eric's first sea voyage thus became a very long one, particularly as the vessel could barely manage ten knots, but by keeping out of the shipping lanes they avoided the U-boats to discover on their belated arrival at Cape Town that their ship was one of only six survivors from those that had left Liverpool nearly two months previously. During a fearful passage the majority had been picked off one by one as they steamed slowly south off the African coast. By contrast morale and general spirit on Eric's boat had been high, supported by enjoyable weather and the discovery by the crew – while seeking to augment fast-diminishing rations from their cargo – that a large proportion of it was wine and spirits intended for the officers' messes of Cairo. This might be seen as a herald of the good luck that was to attend Eric throughout the war.

In Cape Town Eric's duties as a batman terminated and he was billeted at the YMCA to await a shipboard posting. For several days he was told to wait until he was finally directed to a vessel – he could have hardly expected a gleaming white Canadian Pacific cruise ship carrying a full complement of mainly American passengers bound for the Caribbean and Bermuda. As the ship headed out into the South Atlantic with all lights blazing and luxury services operating normally, Eric, having witnessed at close-quarters the sudden, shattering shock of detonating torpedoes, could not help but feel nervous as that familiar phrase 'don't you know there's a war on' ran through his head. But a high-speed Atlantic crossing preceding a leisurely progress through a relaxed itinerary of tropical ports proved wonderfully calming to a man who in his earlier life could never have imagined such comforts.

Disembarking in Bermuda, Eric rendezvoused with his first warship, the light Town-class cruiser HMS *Newcastle,* which was to remain his posting for the next two years. Not that this was to signal an end to his comfortable war: far from it, for the *Newcastle* was on passage to New England for a three-month refit after extended service chasing blockade-runners in the South Atlantic. Within a week Eric was sitting with his shipmates in a New England diner wondering at the complexity of the extensive menu. Settling for a reasonably familiar-sounding mixed grill, he was taken aback – despite his gastronomic experiences aboard the Canadian cruise ship – by the sheer amount of food placed before him, ranging from a large, rare steak to a stack of pancakes.

In December the *Newcastle* was still in the dockyard at Lowell, Massachusetts and Eric, on leave, had decided to go out for the day on a coach trip organised for visiting crews. Returning to the base in the late afternoon, he was astonished to see, standing guard beside a British destroyer, a man he had not seen for two years but who, previous to that, he had spoken to more or less every day. Billy Aldous lived in a council house at Gorseview, Knodishall, adjoining the one that Eric's family had moved to in 1937. The men had been friends when Billy left to join the Royal Navy at the outbreak of war. Eric banged on the window as the bus passed Billy, who looked up to see his old mate and neighbour waving madly. After the sudden surprise a laughing smile creased his face before he pursued the bus at a run to its stopping place. As Eric stepped down the two men grasped each other enthusiastically. After the briefest of explanations of how they each came to be there Billy interjected 'But have you heard?' 'What?' queried Eric. 'The Japs – they've attacked America. Blown up the bloody Yank navy!' It was the evening of Sunday 7 December 1941.

Chinese Adventure

As in Massachusetts Eric Goodwin and Billy Aldous exchanged thoughts on the implications of the Pearl Harbour attack, at Mill House George Thorpe was poking the last embers of the fire before going up to bed. He had just written a lengthy letter to Jack, now serving as a stoker on a motor torpedo boat with the 2nd MTB Flotilla, Royal Navy, based in Hong Kong. He wrote with the news that a few days before, Anne had sent a cake for Florrie's fiftieth birthday on 4 December, remarkable for the fact that this was the first birthday cake Florrie had had in twenty-five years! Clearly he had not heard the latest news from the Far East that, simultaneously with the attack on Pearl Harbour, the Japanese had launched an assault to take Hong Kong. Jack's situation was extremely perilous.

The British government had realised well before the outbreak of war that should the Japanese make a determined move against Hong Kong, it could not be held for long. This thinking was encouraged by Japan's success in its war against China which, with the fall of Canton in 1938, brought the Japanese to the edge of the New Territories, Hong Kong's mainland border with China. Later, in early 1941, Churchill stated there was 'not the slightest chance' of holding the outpost should the Japanese attack. In line with this conviction some senior figures in the colony's administration, including the governor of the time, went so far as to say that resistance to an organised invader could only result in pointless bloodshed and that a better alternative would be to declare Hong Kong an open city in the hope of maintaining a degree of status quo.

Yet as wartime events unfolded during the latter part of 1941, a more bullish attitude developed in London, with Churchill perceiving a need to appear in tune with American policy in the Far East. It was decided that Hong Kong, though it could not be held, should be vigorously defended in the event of an attack, in the hope of slowing a Japanese advance and, perhaps more significantly, to show the as yet uncommitted Americans a symbolic steadfastness of purpose in opposing a common threat. It was a policy that was to have bloody consequences for the military and civilian populations of the colony.

In the autumn of 1941, despite the implementation of defence preparations, the jolly social life of Hong Kong continued in a manner reminiscent of the *Titanic's* band playing on as the waters rose. By the first week of December there were intelligence reports of Japanese troops moving all along the border with the New Territories, but these failed to impinge on the schedule of events for Saturday 6 December. Racing was in full swing at the Happy Valley racecourse, a team from the Middlesex Regiment was playing football against the South China Athletic team, and a grand fete took place at Christ's Church in Waterloo Road. The evening saw the usual number of parties and in Kowloon, across the harbour on the mainland, the charity 'Tin Hat Ball' got under way at the Peninsula Hotel with the aim of raising money to buy bombers for the RAF back home. The governor was present, the mood was happy, and the ambitious target of £160,000 seemed as if it might be reached. Then, towards midnight, the party atmosphere was dowsed by the appearance of the tuxedoed figure of T.B. Wilson, president of the American Steamship Line, on the balcony above the dance floor. Wilson called loudly for quiet and, as the band ceased playing and the chatter ebbed, announced 'Any men connected with any ships in the harbour – report aboard for duty. At once!'

In the morning Major-General Maltby, the senior commanding officer of the Hong Kong garrison, was quietly called from his pew in St John's Cathedral by an officer bearing news of imminent attack. Grim-faced, Maltby and other senior staff slipped away from the service to order all units to battle stations in readiness for a resistance that had been officially calculated as capable of lasting for at least ninety days. Some optimistic parties even believed that reinforcements from Singapore and Pearl Harbour, combined with a rumoured advance of the Chinese Nationalists on the Japanese rear, could well deliver victory over the aggressor. Such thinking was encouraged by rumours that, with small stature and poor eyesight, Japanese troops were incapable of fighting at night and, though capable of beating the Chinese, would be no match for Allied troops.

Facts quickly delivered a harsher reality when news arrived of the loss of most of the US Pacific Fleet at Pearl Harbour and of the sinking of the battleships HMS *Prince of Wales* and HMS *Repulse* by Japanese bombers on 10 December. It was also now clear that no help could be expected from Singapore, itself under threat, and there was no concrete news of a Nationalist advance. Additionally, if there was any fault with the calibre of troops, it was on the Allied side where Indian and British units – softened by years of garrison duty – were allied with newly-recruited and untested Canadian men. Many of the latter were French-speaking and, apart from difficulties with verbal communication, were to have visual problems differentiating between the Chinese allies and Japanese enemy. These defenders now found themselves pitted against ferociously-motivated Japanese soldiers hardened by years of war in China and equipped with meticulously detailed instructions and who, far from being inferior night-fighters, excelled at it.

At 8am on Monday 8 December, a Japanese air raid destroyed the RAF's token presence of two Walrus flying boats and three ancient Vildebeeste torpedo bombers on the ground at their base near Kowloon. At the same time, Japanese troops began to move toward the line of defence on the mainland known as the Gin Drinkers' Line which, it was hoped, would hold for at least a week. It fell within twenty-four hours and, by the morning of Thursday the 11th, all fixed mainland defences had been overrun. At noon Maltby ordered the withdrawal of all troops to Hong Kong Island.

As news of the British evacuation spread through Kowloon it precipitated a complete collapse of order. The chaos – fuelled by fear and a revolt against British authority – was encouraged both by looting Triad gangsters and Fifth Column Japanese sympathisers. Panic-stricken Chinese massed on the quaysides that were being rocked by bomb blasts as enemy aircraft continued to attack ships and gun positions, while artillery shells from the advancing ground troops began to spread carnage through the packed streets. In the harbour Jack Thorpe was with the motor torpedo boats which, together with all other available craft, were engaged in a frantic ferrying of personnel across to the island. The evacuation continued through the night with the final craft to leave the next morning coming under fire, not from the Japanese but from a British machine gun captured and manned by Chinese Triad members installed on the roof of the Kowloon post office.

Similar disaster seemed ready to engulf the island when, as the evacuation from Kowloon was underway on the night of the 11th, intelligence reports revealed a Triad plan to massacre all Europeans on the island during the night of 13 December. The British immediately consulted the Nationalist Chinese who, since the Japanese invasion of China, had established a considerable underground infrastructure in Hong Kong led by the one-legged Admiral Chan Chak. The Admiral, with the official blessing of the Nationalist premier Chiang Kai-Shek, had been quietly assisting with the colony's defence arrangements for some time. He now arranged a meeting with some 200 Triad representatives in the dining room of the Cecil Hotel where it was agreed during the early hours of the 12th that, in return for a large sum of money, the massacre would be cancelled. Blackmail of the British government it might have been, but the situation demanded pragmatism before political squeamishness.

With one immediate danger averted, Chan Chak turned to the next – his more usual business of eliminating Japanese sympathisers from amongst the Chinese population on the island. These 'Fifth Columnists' were actively seeking to aid the invaders by signalling the position of defensive installations, sabotaging vehicles and generally hindering the defenders. They now found their numbers shrinking overnight as the Admiral stepped up the scale of his operations with the recruitment of 2,000 more Chinese whose suitability was assessed less by their business and social background than by their competence in the darkened streets. This very effective group traded as the Loyal and Righteous Charitable Association and within a day or two had increased its membership to 15,000 men, the main attraction being a food allowance of HK$2 a day.

The Admiral, with his diminutive stature and wooden peg-leg, had endeared himself to the British authorities, not only on account of his unfailing efficiency in dealing with all matters involving the Chinese, but also because of his unshakeable cheeriness and calm in the face of calamity. On the night of 12 December his under-cover destruction of an irritating ship-based Japanese propaganda unit broadcasting through loudspeakers from Kowloon was typical of helpful services provided. Consequently the British, grateful for the assistance of the Nationalists against Fifth Columnists, had informally assured Chiang Kai-Shek that they would not allow the Admiral, nor his second-in-command, Colonel Yee, to fall into the hands of the Japanese which would have been a disaster for all parties, not least for the Admiral. This undertaking was to prove the catalyst for some unexpected adventure.

With or without the assistance of sympathetic civilian artillery spotters, a ferocious bombardment of the island from across the harbour continued as the preliminary to an assault. British guns responded in kind, although the heaviest batteries could not be brought to bear: before the war they had been installed facing out to the open sea to protect the colony from threats which, it was assumed, would manifest themselves as naval assaults from that quarter. On the morning of the 13th a launch carrying three Japanese officers set out to cross to the island from Kowloon under the protection of a white flag inscribed 'Peace Mission' and, additionally, of a human/canine shield in the bows formed by two European women with two small dogs. The Japanese, unsure of British etiquette, but conscious of their reputation as dog-lovers, apparently suspected that although it might be considered acceptable to sacrifice women to the vagaries of war, pets were another matter. The officers delivered a politely worded letter from Lieutenant General Sakai, the Japanese commander, suggesting an eminently sensible 'surrender with honour'. But Sakai had not realised the extent of British honour, pride, stubbornness or instruction from London. Governor Young politely declined the offer, as he did again when the Japanese sent a second invitation to surrender on the 17th, adding rather crisply on that occasion that any further envoys would be shot.

Subsequently, during the night of the 17th, four Japanese swimmers slipped quietly across the harbour to reconnoitre landing sites on the island. The following night 7,500 troops came ashore from every sort of craft that could be found and began driving a north-south wedge to split the island's defences in two. Again it quickly became clear that any arrogant assumptions about the enemy's night-fighting capabilities had been just that. The defence soon became hopeless though extremely tenacious, which encouraged the loss of any semblance of discipline or honourable conduct on the part of the invaders. The horror of close combat ran the whole bloody gamut of atrocity. Disarmed prisoners were deliberately maimed, tortured and bayoneted. The wounded were bayoneted in their hospital beds. Medical staff were coldly executed. Nurses were raped, disfigured and murdered atop piles of bloody corpses.

On 21 December Governor Young, advised by General Maltby that virtually all was lost, cabled London for permission to agree terms. The cable crossed with one from Churchill:

> There must be no thought of surrender. Every part of the Island must be fought over and the enemy resisted with the utmost stubbornness. Every day that you are able to maintain your resistance you help the Allied cause all over the world.

The austere and upright Young carried on, outwardly jaunty with swinging Malacca cane and perfectly polished shoes, but inwardly sick as the slaughter continued towards its inevitable conclusion.

At this point Admiral Chan Chak repeated an earlier offer to use the vigilantes of the Loyal and Righteous Charitable Association as frontline troops if the British would arm them. A plan was also put forward by the Chinese intellectual Liang Shuming, encouraged by an independent free-thinking Englishwoman, Elsie Fairfax Cholmondely, that messages should be sent to Chiang Kai-Shek advocating he send his airforce and speed up the advance of the Nationalist Army as a relief column. The British demurred on two counts: uneasiness at the thought of equipping the dubiously qualified membership of the Loyal and Righteous with modern automatic weapons; and secondly, a political undercurrent of thought which suggested that, although Hong Kong would be recoverable from the Japanese in due course, things might not be so straightforward if they were rescued by the Chinese. By the time it was agreed, in extremis, to allow Chan Chak some weaponry, it was Christmas Eve and too late.

On the morning of Christmas Day Governor Young issued a Christmas message to the few remaining defenders.

> In pride and admiration I send my greeting to all who are fighting and all who are working so nobly and so well to sustain Hong Kong against the assaults of the enemy. Fight on. Hold fast for King and Empire. God bless you all in this your finest hour … The Order of the Day is to hold fast.

The bombing, bombardment, hand-to-hand fighting and bloody atrocities continued through the day with all units, and the Governor, heroically prepared to resist to the last man in accordance with Churchill's orders. But by mid-afternoon Maltby insisted to Young that it was pointless to continue. After further deliberation the Governor reluctantly conceded and at 3.25pm orders were issued to cease fighting. In the early evening the two men presented themselves to the Japanese and were ferried across the harbour to General Sakai's HQ in the Peninsula Hotel. Here, by candlelight, Young signed a document of unconditional surrender, the first surrender of a British colony since the American War of Independence.

Despite the withdrawal to Singapore of the destroyers *Scout* and *Thanet* on the evening of the first day of fighting, the Royal Navy had played a heroic part in the defence of the colony with those vessels and personnel retained on base. These were the destroyer HMS

Thracian, five gunboats, the eight motor torpedo boats of the 2nd MTB Flotilla with which Jack Thorpe was serving, and a handful of auxiliary craft. Jack was one of the crew on MTB 11 which, on 11 December, was engaged in the hurried evacuation from Kowloon after the rout of the mainland forces. Sustaining damage during the operation, she was obliged to return to the Aberdeen dockyard on the south side of the island to be hoisted out for repairs. By the evening of the 15th she was back in service, unluckily for MTB 08 which, waiting her turn for repairs to her propeller, was hoisted onto the slip that night only to be totally destroyed during an air raid on the dockyard the following day.

On the 19th – as Japanese troops continued to press across the harbour to the island – the seven remaining MTBs were ordered into the attack. No more dramatic account of that action can be given than that contained in the barely measured tones of the subsequent report from the commander of MTB 07, Lieutenant R. R. W. Ashby.

At 08.45 on Friday December 19th, 1941, acting on instructions received through you from XDO to Proceed into Harbour and shoot anything inside I slipped ROBIN and proceeded with the other MTB in my subdivision from Aberdeen into East Lamma Channel through Sulphur Channel into the Harbour at 30 knots. With 09 keeping station one cable astern I proceeded along the outside of the boat boom and passed the Naval Dockyard. On nearing North Point I came under heavy machine-gun fire and this was my first indication that the Japanese had actually landed and established themselves on Hong Kong Island. I continued towards Kowloon Bay and sighted numbers of landing craft in threes crossing from East of Holt's Wharf and making for the area west of Tai Koo Sugar Refinery. These landing craft which appeared very frail (probably portable) were in threes towed by the leading boat of each three which had an outboard motor. Each boat contained from 12 to 15 men.

I immediately signalled to 09 to attack independently and increasing to full speed (37 knots) I went in to attack. Aircraft now started diving on me with machine-gun and cannon fire.

I opened fire on the landing craft with all five Lewis guns at 100yards range, with excellent effect, and passed down the leading string at a distance of about five yards, firing continuously. I dropped two depth charges which failed to explode owing to insufficient depth of water. However this made no difference as the landing craft capsized in my wash and there appeared to be no survivors.

I then came under machine-gun fire from both shores and from wrecks in the harbour, from howitzers, and light artillery fire from both shores, also from cannon and machine-gun fire from aircraft. The boat was hit several times and a cannon shell exploded in the engine room, putting the starboard engine out of action and killing the leading Stoker. I ordered the telegraphist to the engine room to investigate. My speed was reduced to 22 knots. However I turned and attacked a second bunch of landing craft with machine-gun fire at point-blank range with most satisfactory effect. Another cannon shell now put my port engine out of action and my telegraphist was killed by machine-gun fire. My speed was reduced to 12 knots and I was making water in the engine-room, so I had no alternative but to try and extricate myself and endeavour to reach my Base. I headed for the Naval Yard under intense machine-gun and howitzer fire and under attack from three aircraft. I directed fire against the diving aircraft and tracers were observed to enter the fuselage of two of them, one of which made off towards Kowloon low down and did not return. After passing the Naval Dockyard firing slackened off, 09 rejoined then and I was able to leave Harbour by Sulphur Channel. After rounding Mount Davis my centre and last engine gave out and I ordered 09 to take me in tow. The crew were able to plug most of the bullet holes below the water line and by pumping it was possible to keep the boat afloat.

I secured alongside ROBIN at 10.00 and was able to repair all damage except one torpedo rail which had been severed by a shell. In addition to landing craft and aircraft, Japanese on wrecks in the harbour were also machine-gunned.

MTBs 11 and 12 followed 07 and 09 into the attack. Both were hit by sustained fire. With Jack Thorpe still alive in its engine room, MTB

11 was forced to withdraw after six of her crew were killed but MTB 12, taking a direct shell hit to her bridge, crashed into the Kowloon seawall at full speed with the loss of all but one of her nine crew. With the realisation that further attack would be suicidal, MTBs 10, 26 and 27 were recalled but in the heat of the action MTB 26 missed the signal and continued to press on. She was last seen stopped off North Point, her crew all dead.

The five surviving MTBs retired to the relative safety of Aberdeen on the south coast although the dockyard was now under increasing attack from aircraft and artillery. On 21 December MTB 10 was riddled with bomb splinters during an air raid which sank the gunboat HMS *Cicala*, but the only premature fatality on MTB 10 was a duck planned for Christmas dinner, a festive event which, even given the extreme stoicism of the Royal Navy, was beginning to look inappropriate. As the situation in the Aberdeen dockyard became more dangerous the MTBs moved to a position in the lee of the small offshore island of Apleichou which gave some protection from artillery fire. Here they lurked under camouflage during daylight hours, hoping to avoid air attacks until darkness allowed cautious patrolling of the island's seaward coastline.

As the inevitable approached during the morning of Christmas Day, Admiral Chan Chak and Colonel Yee realised the time had come to make a speedy departure. A request to the British for help in providing some sort of escape vessel resulted in an agreement that the MTBs would be made available to evacuate the Admiral and his party together with a handful of senior British intelligence officers. The plan was for this group to rendezvous with the MTBs at Aberdeen that afternoon. Unfortunately in the chaos of the day the Navy had not been made aware of the importance of the Admiral's escape and, assuming normal rules would apply, was more concerned to get the MTBs away before a surrender placed that option out of order.

On MTB 10 Lieutenant-Commander Gandy, the commanding officer of the 2nd MTB Flotilla, had already taken on board three high-priority secret service men, the senior being F.W. Kendall who had been operating in China prior to the Japanese advance on Hong Kong. At 3.15pm, just before the order to surrender was released, Gandy received an order from Fortress HQ on the island 'Go all boats'. Impressed by Kendall of the need to wait for Chan Chak, Gandy signalled back a request that his departure be delayed until darkness provided cover from attack and by when, hopefully, the Admiral would have shown up. The response from Fortress HQ was to repeat the earlier order and, just in case the signal was failing to get through, Lieutenant-Commander Yorath was ordered to get down to Aberdeen, find the MTBs and repeat the order personally to Gandy.

At this point a group of six men being the Admiral, Colonel Yee, the Admiral's *aide-de-camp* Henry Heng Hsu, his bodyguard Yeung Chuen, and two British officers were in an old Austin convertible commandeered by Henry Heng Hsu and now attempting a passage through Japanese lines to Aberdeen. Various Japanese patrols and road-blocks were negotiated by dint of Henry keeping his hand hard down on the horn and his foot hard down on the accelerator while yelling loudly in Japanese 'Banzai! Long live the Emperor!' every time they approached a potentially hostile situation. In such a manner they managed to reach Aberdeen with only a few desultory shots having been fired after them. Here they encountered a number of other British officers who had just arrived in a Buick, and also a number of Navy personnel including Commander Hugh Montague who was hoping to re-float the tug C410 which had run aground that morning. A small motor launch, tender to the auxiliary *Cornflower*, was found and loaded with fuel and supplies with the intention of ferrying the party out to the back of Apleichou Island to look for the MTBs. Montague with six or seven seamen would stay behind to re-float the tug which, it was planned, would pick up the first party after dark if in fact the MTBs had already left.

Lieutenant-Commander Yorath now arrived from HQ to make sure that the MTBs had left. Montague advised him of events saying that if the boats had not gone they would be behind Apleichou Island, whereon Yorath decided to take a ship's lifeboat lying nearby and row across, helped by one of the seamen. Gunfire from the Japanese forced them to abort their first attempt, but on the second they got across without injury to find MTB 10 sheltering behind the lee shore. Going aboard, Yorath forcefully repeated the order to leave immediately while Kendall argued the case for saving the Admiral and Gandy, as officer-in-charge, considered his course. At this point all three men were unaware that the Admiral was already involved in a near-death situation.

Unfortunately for those aboard her, the *Cornflower's* boat had unadvisedly left the Aberdeen dockyard via the east channel between Hong Kong Island and Apleichau Island rather than via the west channel. This course soon brought them within sight and range of the machine gun in Pillbox 12 on the beach below Brick Hill which had been taken by the Japanese. The first bursts killed two seamen, hit another in both legs and riddled the boat, setting fire to the engine. Stopped dead and under fire there was no alternative for the survivors but to jump, at which point Colonel Yee let it be known that he couldn't swim. The Admiral had already given his life-jacket to Yeung Cheun – who also could not swim – so, unable to help the Colonel, he unstrapped his wooden leg preparatory to jumping overboard. The HK$40,000 which he had taken the precaution of secreting inside it against later emergencies fluttered away on the gentle evening breeze. 'What shall we do?' the Admiral asked of the ever-resourceful Henry Heng Hsu. Henry, a Christian, for once at a loss for practical advice replied 'Pray! Pray to God!' 'Right' exclaimed the Admiral, a Buddhist, 'if we get out of this I shall convert to your religion!' and jumped into the sea.

The Japanese continued firing as the swimmers struggled toward Apleichau Island through a shoal of Portuguese men-of-war, a minor hazard in the circumstances. The wounded seaman was drowning noisily, David MacDougall (Head of the Department of Information) took a bullet in the back of his shoulder and Admiral Chan Chak was hit in the wrist. The exhausted men struggled onto the rocks of the shoreline still observed through binoculars by the Japanese who now directed some light artillery pieces to finish off the job. Rock splinters and shrapnel whined around the men until darkness brought respite and an opportunity to cross to the south side of the island in search of the MTBs. Henry Heng Hsu left the Admiral, weak from loss of blood, with a Bible and a pistol, primarily for self-destruction, in case the Japanese decided to cross the channel to investigate.

On reaching a high point on the island the party were exhilarated to make out in the luminous darkness a motor torpedo boat lying just offshore. Removing their shirts to use as signalling flags they jumped and shouted on the skyline, only to be answered by a burst of fire from MTB10's Lewis guns, having been mistaken for Japanese. MTB10 then weighed anchor and moved further offshore, presumably to lessen the risk from returning small arms fire. Though further swimming was the last thing any of the party had hoped for, a naval cadet, Holger Christiansen, volunteered to swim out to the MTB. Dragged aboard he blurted out 'There're ten chaps following me!' whereon the MTB's Lewis guns opened up again, the crew having thought he had said 'ten Japs'. Luckily no casualties were inflicted and the rest of the party were picked up in skiffs from the other four MTBs which had now joined Gandy.

Henry Heng Hsu, with a seaman from MTB10, immediately set off back to the island in a skiff to retrieve the Admiral but found he was not where he had been left. After a desperate search he returned to MTB10. Lieutenant-Commander Yorath and Bill Robinson, a senior figure in the Indian police, then volunteered to continue the search and eventually found the Admiral in a poor way higher up the island. Bringing him back in the skiff they thought it strange that he crossed himself while propped up in the stern, not realising that, in compliance with his undertaking to Henry Heng Hsu, he had already decided on a conversion to Christianity and, further, to change his first name to Andrew.

Once aboard MTB10 the Admiral began to revive amid the general jollity of the improved circumstances and, with his wound dressed and Gandy's naval cap stuck jauntily on his head, advised the Commander to shape course for Mirs Bay, 100 miles to the northeast. At 9.30pm, in a mounting crescendo of noise, the five MTBs throttled up their 1,500 horse-power engines to full speed and roared seaward line astern at thirty knots. Lieutenant Ashby on MTB07 could see his house ablaze on the hill above Aberdeen.

The Admiral's plan was to land on the Chinese coast in an area as yet not fully occupied by the Japanese and from there to escape into the mainland interior to join up with the Nationalist forces. As the MTBs did not have the range to reach friendly territory towards Singapore in the south the British were happy to place themselves in the hands of the Admiral whose local knowledge, they realised, provided the best chance of escape.

The five MTBs arrived off the small inhabited island of Ping Chau in Mirs Bay in the early hours after a brief encounter with a Japanese destroyer in the dark. Under cover of the flotilla's Lewis guns, Kendall and Yeung Chuen were rowed ashore with instructions from the Admiral to seize the local headman and return him to the boat for interrogation as to Japanese dispositions. The Admiral was by now dressed in Gandy's spare uniform to complement the cap and with his arm in a sling looked quite the Nelsonian figure despite his small size and one leg. Relaxed by a shot of rum and hot cocoa the villager brought aboard proved more than cooperative with details of Japanese movements and the location of anti-Japanese partisans on the mainland. Consequently, after returning him to the shore and taking onboard one or two fishermen as pilots, the MTBs moved slowly off in close formation towards the village of Namoa a few miles distant on the mainland coast. On approaching Namoa a sudden alert brought the Lewis guns to bear on the dark outline of a largish vessel lying just offshore. A quick exchange of shouted oaths and ribaldry revealed this to be the tug C410 bearing Commander Montague and six others who by good fortune had chosen the same landfall, although their vessel was once again aground.

Helping the party ashore was a band of guerrillas under the control of Leung Wing Yuen who greeted the Admiral enthusiastically. The boats were stripped of supplies and anything else that might be useful to the escape party or the guerrillas before being moved out into the bay to be scuttled. With only twelve feet of water under them this operation was not entirely successful, leaving the boats visible to the Japanese as evidence of the escape route and presenting the risk of brutal retribution for the people of the nearby villages. But with daylight approaching the urgency was to get away from the coast. Kendall as the senior 'China' man took control of the whole group of seventy men, the majority being the crews of the MTBs, Jack Thorpe among them. Most were dressed in white navy sweaters and various oddments salvaged from the naval stores piled on the beach. Each man was instructed to carry a weapon, ammunition and as much food as could be managed. The Admiral was provided with a chair lashed between two bamboo carrying poles and an escort of fierce-looking guerrillas. An hour before dawn the party set off upwards into the hills with the Admiral at the front and the rest following behind in a long single file, the sailors feeling particularly apprehensive and some a little disgruntled at the loss of their ships. The villagers lined the path, enthusiastically cheering this desperate-looking column at the start of a 3,000-mile journey across China.

After three miles they stopped on a low ridge. The Admiral and Leung Wing Yuen had decided daylight movement on the coast was likely to be observed from the sea or air. As the sun rose on a perfect day, Namoa Bay shimmered flatly in the morning light below them, the scuttled MTBs starkly visible under the clear water. The exhausted men, a few of whom were especially surprised and grateful to still be alive, took cover in the trees and rested through the day before resuming the march in the late afternoon. The going was rough, through steeply mountainous country over faint and precipitous tracks which, without the guidance of the Chinese guerrillas, the group could never have negotiated.

During a rest break these guerrillas, curious to test the famed prowess of the Royal Navy, suggested a shooting match. Gandy took careful aim with his pistol at a crow conveniently perched nearby and squeezed off a round only to hear a slight pop as the damp cartridge failed to detonate. It did, however, manage to set off great hilarity amongst the guerrillas who were probably encouraged to take their

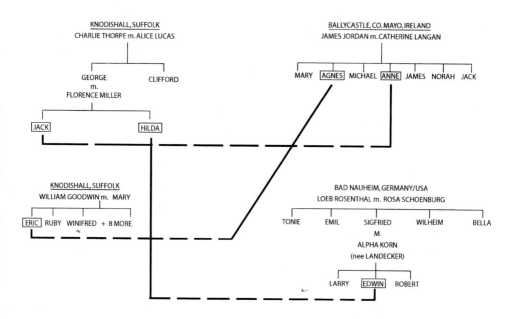

KNODISHALL, SUFFOLK
CHARLIE THORPE m. ALICE LUCAS

BALLYCASTLE, CO. MAYO, IRELAND
JAMES JORDAN m. CATHERINE LANGAN

GEORGE
m.
FLORENCE MILLER

CLIFFORD

MARY AGNES MICHAEL ANNE JAMES NORAH JACK

JACK

HILDA

KNODISHALL, SUFFOLK
WILLIAM GOODWIN m. MARY

BAD NAUHEIM, GERMANY/USA
LOEB ROSENTHAL m. ROSA SCHOENBURG

ERIC RUBY WINIFRED + 8 MORE

TONIE EMIL SIGFRIED WILHEIM BELLA
M.
ALPHA KORN
(nee LANDECKER)

LARRY EDWIN ROBERT

Three wartime weddings.

Mill House, Knodishall.

Charlie and Alice Thorpe in later years.

Siegfried and Alpha Rosenthal.

Florrie.

George (third from left, holding his hat) in the British Army.

George and Florrie are married 5 February 1918. Charlie and Alice, George's parents, front row left.

Jack and Hilda Thorpe.

Florrie, George, Charlie, and Alice Thorpe between the wars.

1937 — POLICE PASS

EDW. ROSENTHAL

IS A MEMBER OF THE

BUFFALO TIMES

Please Assist Him as Your Duty Permits

COMMISSIONER OF POLICE

MANAGING EDITOR

Ed Rosenthal: 1937 Press Pass.

Eric Goodwin.

The Hong Kong Escape Group. Jack Thorpe is hatless, second row from back, behind left shoulder of a man wearing an officer's cap and white scarf. (The Waichow photograph)

陳中委策將軍率領香港陸海空軍官兵由港突圍脫逃惠川留影 民三十年十二月廿九日 29TH DEC. 1941

ADMIRAL CHEN CHAK WITH BRITISH OFFICERS AND MEN WHOM HIS EXCELLENCY LED THROUGH THE JAPANESE LINES AFTER THE FALL OF HONG KONG AND ARRIVED SAFELY AT WAICHOW

Jack and Florrie at Mill House.

Anne Jordan.

HMS *Mahratta*.

Anne Jordan becomes Mrs Anne Thorpe. Agnes Jordan is behind the little boy in the sailor outfit.

Jack Thorpe.

Ed (on the left) with officers, ground crew and P51 Mustang.

Hilda.

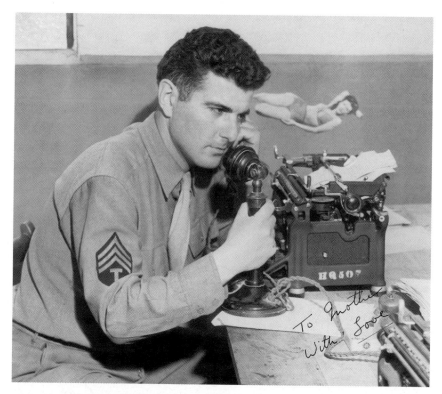

Ed shows mother what the day job is all about.

7 July 1945.

Au revoir.

Ed and Hilda are married.

protection duties even more seriously thereafter. Jack would later recall Gandy's embarrassment at this failure of naval firepower.

The next day, the 27 December, the party came up to their first serious obstacle, the main coast road heavily trafficked by the Japanese. With cautious scouting and signalling, and continuing bribes to keep the local banditry sweet, the guerrillas managed to shepherd the party across without detection including, by this stage, a second sedan chair required for the injured David MacDougall. By midnight they had covered over thirty miles and, exhausted, slept out in intense cold under cover of an orchard.

After a further sixteen miles on the 28th all were greatly relieved to encounter columns of Nationalist Chinese troops moving back to their bases after abandoning their southward march towards Hong Kong on hearing of the British surrender. The Nationalist advance had not been purely rumour! The situation continued to improve on the 29th when, after another long march of over twenty miles, the escapees approached the Nationalist-held town of Waichow. Enthusiastically helpful on learning of the approach of the Royal Navy, the townsfolk sent out bicycles pedalled by locals to pick up stragglers suffering from blistered feet and other ailments. Unfortunately, although the gesture was appreciated, the rough and rocky nature of the track prevented this operation delivering much relief.

Eventually the column collected itself together on the edge of the town. Straightening their backs and hats the men fell in, determined to make the land-locked town's first view of the Navy as impressive a one as could be managed in the circumstances: usual standards could not be hoped for with no two men dressed alike and all carrying nearly a week's growth of beard. Behind the White Ensign and the Chinese flag carried side by side they marched past the town's Chief Magistrate in the central square and on to an ex-German mission hospital where the Chinese Army provided them with an expansive traditional banquet.

In the morning all gathered for a group photograph in front of the mission before attending a service in the mission church. Here the British sat quietly mystified as a Chinese official ranted unintelligibly before apparently calling for the Chinese national anthem. All stood up and the British tried gallantly to hum along with the singing. Commander Montague then addressed the congregation with praise and gratitude for the hospitality and help of the Chinese and followed with encouragement for the war effort. He then called for the British national anthem although, embarrassingly, nobody could remember any words beyond the first verse. The solemnity of this rendition of 'God Save the King' was not much helped by Jack with two of the other ratings providing musical accompaniment using their combs as kazoos.

On New Year's Eve the party embarked on four seventy-foot river barges, two powered with primitive charcoal engines pulling the other two. Speed was around two knots. Over five days these barges moved 150 miles up the often crowded East River, their irregular cargo keeping well hidden when passing through occasional areas controlled by the Japanese. Reaching Lungchun they were met by a British colonel, Owen Hughes, who had been on the last plane to get out of Hong Kong and was now working with the Nationalist Army. Leaving the guerrilla escort on the river, Hughes organised five trucks, with a car for the Admiral and MacDougall, to take the party 200 miles on to Kukong where they arrived on 8 January. Here the ailing Admiral was taken into a Welsh Methodist mission hospital to have the bullet removed from his wrist. Subsequently he had it mounted on a gold chain to wear as a lapel badge.

In Kukong the party received news that was unanimously depressing: the situation in Singapore was grim, Burma was under attack and, on a more personal level, word came that the Japanese were attempting to raise the MTBs and had massacred many of the villagers who had assisted with the getaway. Further, the Japanese propagandist 'Tokyo Rose' was announcing in radio broadcasts that the authorities were well aware of the escape route and were about to seize the escapees. Accommodation for the men was provided aboard a spacious houseboat which normally served as the town's brothel but which Henry Heng Hsu had arranged to rent for their stay, *sans* staff.

Commander Montague as the senior naval officer, with seven other senior army and civilian personnel, was now ordered to fly north to report on the fall of Hong Kong at the British embassy in the Nationalist capital of Chungking. Kendall with the two other secret service men had remained behind in Waichow and, with the Admiral in hospital attended by his two colleagues, Gandy was left in command of the fifty or so Navy men remaining. Loaded with Chinese dollars provided by Hughes to expedite their onward journey, this group continued by rail towards Burma, but not before being beaten 8-0 in a football match against a Chinese team from the Kukong YMCA. After five days and 750 miles by train they reached the railhead on 21 January, but with Lieutenant Ashby seriously ill with typhoid. Four trucks were procured to take them on westward through the mountains over tortuous roads which saw one of the trucks overturn when coasting too fast downhill, putting three sailors in the local hospital at Kweiyang with broken limbs. At Kweiyang the group was provided with Red Cross ambulances for the 1,000-mile journey over the Burma Road to the Burmese border. After another two weeks of hair-raising travel over the high mountains at the eastern extremity of the Himalayas they reached the British lines of the Burma Frontier Force, whose men were more than a little surprised to see a contingent of the Royal Navy emerging from the Chinese interior.

Throughout their journey across China the group had been impressed to a man by the unfailing hospitality, helpfulness and stoicism of the ordinary people who, despite their own extreme poverty of food and resources so exacerbated by destructive Japanese attacks, displayed a resolute cheerfulness and generosity of spirit. The noble qualities of the Admiral and his colleagues had also made a deep impression on the British, their gratitude emphasised in Montague's report of the escape which lead to the subsequent awards of KBE to the Admiral and OBE to Henry Heng Hsu.

At the border the group entrained for Mandalay and Rangoon, arriving in the Burmese capital on Valentine's Day, 1942. Any thought that their epic journey had brought them to safety was immediately destroyed by orders that they were to be deployed in the defence of the city against an unexpected Japanese thrust from the south. It seemed as if it would be Hong Kong all over again. But this time the more than hopeless state of Rangoon's defences, combined with Australia's refusal to commit forces to an irrecoverable situation, encouraged an early departure, and those of the Hong Kong party who had not been assigned as gun crew to armed merchantmen were relieved to sail for India on 23 February. Their dismay was intense when, a few hours later, their ship was ordered back to Rangoon: it had been decided to attempt a defence after all. Then, on 8 March, policy was reversed again in the face of the rapid Japanese advance and the Hong Kong party left harbour on the requisitioned Danish freighter *Heinrich Jessen* which had previously escaped both Hong Kong and Singapore, the latter having fallen on 15 February. Rangoon lay deserted under dense clouds of oily black smoke rising from the oil refineries and depots, the demolition parties having done their work. Two hours later the Japanese 21st Armoured Regiment was able to enter the city without a shot being fired.

The *Heinrich Jessen* reached Calcutta on 12 March. What was left of the Royal Navy group now crossed India by train to Bombay and, with survivors from the *Prince of Wales* and *Repulse*, boarded the *Narkunda* for Durban, Cape Town, Freetown and Glasgow. After loading 500 Italian POWs in Durban they sailed on to Capetown, arriving on 12 April. They sailed for home on the 19th but engine trouble forced a return to Table Bay to facilitate repairs. On 28 April *Narkunda* continued her journey, eventually docking in Glasgow late in the afternoon of Friday 22 May 1942. On board were thirty-one men from the original escape party including A/B Stoker Jack Thorpe, ex. MTB11.

On 9 January a brief item had appeared in the *Daily Express* from a Chungking source reporting the names of the escape party, the information having been conveyed to the embassy there by Montague and the other senior officers. In St Albans Hilda, scanning the paper for any news from the Far East, gasped with relief at seeing her brother's name on the list, for the public were by now well aware of the comprehensive calamity in Hong Kong. She immediately sent a telegram to Mill House with a promise to forward the paper. Yet the relief felt by the family was extinguished ten days later when an official letter arrived from the Commodore in Devonport stating that Jack was missing on war service and implying that the worst must be feared. That fear gathered strength with the passing weeks and months as no further word was received of Jack's survival. After such early hope Florrie, George, Hilda and not least Annie, were distraught and, though outwardly refusing to give up hope, each was inwardly becoming resigned to the loss as the weeks went by.

The truth was that Jack had no intention of tempting fate by sending any messages home until safely back on British soil. He had seen too many ships go down to assume that the *Narkunda* would arrive safely. And in any event it was in his nature to enjoy surprising people. So it was that on Sunday afternoon, 24 May 1942, Florrie looked up from washing the dishes to see through the window, in his Navy uniform, her only son opening the garden gate, smiling from ear to ear.

Hitting Back in the ETO

Back at Mill House Jack Thorpe must have felt that he had left the Japanese war as far away as it could be. Yet the repercussions of Japan's aggressive expansionism were to manifest themselves very close to home when, in September 1942, John Mowlem & Co. began the construction of an airfield on 500 acres of clay farmland just to the north of Knodishall. Forced by the Pearl Harbour attack to an immediate declaration of war, the US now stood shoulder to shoulder with Britain against Japan in the Pacific and against Germany in what it termed the European Theatre of Operations. And by now it was more than clear to the strategists that heavy investment in the developing technologies of air power was an essential first step in the defeat of the Axis forces.

Although aircraft had been used aggressively in World War I, it was not until Franco's bombers inflicted such terror and carnage on Spain's Republican population that military minds began to appreciate their full potential. If any confirmation was needed, the part played by the vanguard of screaming Stuka dive-bombers heralding Hitler's *blitzkrieg* across Europe was it. Previous thinking had regarded aircraft primarily as a means of supporting ground troops, as in the case of the Stukas, but now the strategists were considering the use of long-range bombers as a means of destroying enemy infrastructure well behind the front lines. Some overly-optimistic proponents of this idea developed the theory that advances in technology would allow an air force to so damage Germany from a distance that an eventual invasion of Europe might merely involve the placement of an occupying force. More important, in Churchill's eyes at least, was that with Germany holding all mainland Europe and Scandinavia and, in 1942, remaining strong in North Africa, a bombing campaign launched from besieged Britain represented virtually the only way of hitting back at the aggressor.

The new bombing strategy was based on the latest four-engined, long-range aircraft, particularly the Boeing B-17 Flying Fortress. These were equipped with a self-regulating oxygen supply for the crew and turbo-chargers for the engines forcing compressed air into the carburettors, together allowing the aircraft to operate at altitudes of up to 30,000 feet (the cruising height of modern passenger jets) and at speeds of 300 miles an hour. The theory maintained that at this height and speed the aircraft would be immune from ground-based anti-aircraft fire and be relatively safe from attacking fighter aircraft, which would, of necessity, be flying at the limits of their capabilities. Just in case, armour and self-sealing fuel tanks were fitted and the plane, as its name suggested, bristled with heavy-calibre machine-guns mounted in hydraulically rotated turrets.

The idea was that the bombers would fly in a close 'box' formation allowing the gunners to release such a barrage of fire at any aircraft foolish enough to attack, from whatever quarter, that the attacker's destruction would be assured. The advanced technical component particularly crucial to the viability of this strategy was the electro-mechanical Norden bombsight which, in trials over the dry Muroc Lake in California, enabled bombardiers to land their projectiles within fifty feet of the target from four miles up, thus beginning the still current doctrine of precision bombing. It all looked wonderfully sound on paper and in the summer of 1942 American bombers and escort fighters began arriving in eastern England after the long flight via Maine, Goose Bay, Greenland, Reykjavik and Prestwick.

The flaw in the theory was that for the bombsight to work properly it was necessary to be able to see the target and, unlike Muroc Lake, north-west Europe was normally covered with cloud. This was often patchy and localised over assembly or target areas making mission planning dependent on weather forecasts with consequent last-minute uncertainty. Dense cloud encountered en route could confuse navigation, hide enemy fighters and occasionally result in catastrophic mid-air collisions. And not least of the disadvantages suffered by the American bombers was the decision, made by those with faith in the theory and a desire to utilise the Norden to best effect, to operate during daylight hours alone.

Other problems had also been underestimated: the inexperience of American air-crews, the accuracy of radar-controlled anti-aircraft fire, and the skill of experienced German fighter pilots who, with their ground controllers, became adept at intercepting the bombers the moment the latter's fighter escort dropped away due to their shorter range. A five-second burst of fire from German fighters attacking line abreast from dead ahead (the quarter least covered by the bombers' guns) would send the wreckage of the big planes spiralling earthward trailing plumes of black smoke, or else vaporise them in mid-air as bombs and fuel detonated. Surviving aircraft would land back in East Anglia riddled with cannon and shrapnel holes; blood-spattered interiors carrying dead, dying and mutilated men, few older than twenty-five.

Losses through the summer of 1943 rose to unacceptable levels. On 14 October, of 291 Fortresses sent to bomb the ball-bearing factories of Schweinfurt, 62 were shot down resulting in over 600 men missing. Another 50 dead and badly wounded men were removed from the returning aircraft and, of these aircraft, 17 were written off,

121 required major repair and only 30 were undamaged. Propaganda called the raid a great victory but the reality was, that with losses running at more than double the ten per cent level the USAAF had previously declared as being prohibitive to continuing operations, the concept of unescorted daylight bombing was as dead as the missing aircrews.

Morale on the bomber bases had touched bottom. Each crew was obliged to complete twenty-five missions before returning home, but in early 1944, with the average life-span of a B-17 standing at only twenty-one missions, statistically the chance of avoiding death or capture was less than nil. Vacant tables in the mess and empty bunks in the Nissen huts on the evening after a mission did not help. Nor did stress arising from the abortion of missions just before take-off, usually as the result of worsening weather. Apart from preventing flying, winter weather could also make life on the bases a misery. The 1940s suffered a succession of extreme winters and the persistent grey skies and damp cold added a particularly depressing element to the lives of men marooned in primitive facilities amid the mud of bleak airfields in a foreign country, itself depressed by four years of war. 'Section Eighted' – indicating a man's psychological breakdown – appeared with increasing frequency in medical records.

By the end of the USAAF's activities in the European Theatre of Operations many of the forty or so bomber 'Groups' of 40–50 aircraft each had lost over 150 aircraft and crews, meaning their whole complement of aircraft had been replaced three or four times over, equating to the loss of around 1,500 men per group. The 381st Bombardment Group, based at Ridgewell in Essex, commenced operations on 22 June 1943 with thirty-six crews of ten men each. Three months later, at the beginning of October, twenty-six crews – seventy-two per cent of those men – had been lost. Ground crews too suffered wear and tear. Personally dedicated to individual aircraft and crew they often worked around the clock to repair damage and keep their 'ship' flying. But, unlike the combat crews, they were given no target of missions to complete, being in for the duration. And to these ground crew fell the task of removing from aircraft interiors the blood and flesh that had been part of friends they might have joked with during boarding in the pre-dawn gloom of that morning.

The problems were largely resolved in 1944 with the appearance of the P-51 Mustang fighter fitted with the Rolls-Royce Merlin engine as in the Spitfire. This long-range aircraft, when equipped with disposable fuel drop-tanks, could make a return flight to Berlin and still have enough fuel left to engage the enemy in high-altitude, high-speed combat in which it had a distinct edge in performance. With this protection in place all the way to the target and back, and re-equipped by booming US manufacturing, the daylight bombing campaign could continue with weight. Soon 1,000-bomber raids became commonplace and losses declined to well below the ten per cent level set as the maximum tolerable.

The deployment of all this air power over Europe required a large infrastructure on the ground and the US Army 8th Air Force eventually occupied 112 stations, most of them airfields newly-constructed in a great arc around the Wash fenlands from Peterborough and Bedford in the west, south to Cambridge and up through Suffolk and Norfolk, where most were located. Of the 200,000 personnel only a small proportion were combat flyers, the majority being engaged in a vast range of support services from command HQs to weather forecasting. Each airfield provided accommodation for 1,500–3,000 men with the various facilities and barracks dispersed around the site to lessen casualties and damage in the event of attack. Most were constructed in the period 1942–43 by civilian contractors employed by the British government before being handed over to the Americans on completion.

The military planners had decided that the Leiston airfield, Station 373, would accommodate fighter aircraft. Ancient oaks and elms were felled and their roots blasted out with dynamite as Mowlem brought in heavy machinery to clear and burn the hedges and fill the ditches in preparation for the laying of five miles of concrete runway and the construction of facilities for 1,700 men and 70–80 fighter planes. Most of the land itself had been requisitioned at £35 per acre from the owner of the 633 acres of Moat and Hill Farms, Leiston who, surprisingly, was Richard Garrett Engineering Works Ltd: the company had bought the properties at £9 per acre when they became vacant early in 1940. Whether this was a case of astute speculation or simply a desire by the management to 'dig for victory' on a scale worthy of the Works, is unknown. Certainly Mr Leek, Garrett's farm foreman at Hill Farm, was dismayed by developments and, deciding that the edge of an airfield to be populated by a thousand or so servicemen was no place to bring up his teenage daughters, moved to a new job in Yoxford five miles away. It is doubtful the girls wanted to miss the excitement.

Any local men not in the Forces and capable of work were employed by 1942, and although the farm-workers might have envied the better wages of the construction workers engaged by Mowlem, the fact of their tied housing in cottages belonging to the farms rendered them unable to do anything about it. Mowlem was thus obliged to import gangs of Irish labourers, adding to the diverse mix of immigrant men already present for defence and training purposes in what had been, until two or three years previously, a quiet rural backwater. Accommodated in a primitive encampment on site and working long hours with only one weekend off in eight, the Irishmen engaged little with the locals but drinking and fighting between themselves was commonplace when opportunity for the former arose.

Nineteen-year-old Joyce Leek, married to the son of Garrett's ex-farm foreman, was still living at home at the Gatehouse, Knodishall where her mother was responsible for manning the gates of the nearest level-crossing to the new airfield. She remembers two Irishmen locked in a violent wrestling match in the centre of the crossing itself, cheered on by an audience of their fellows. Fearful that a train might come at any minute and resolve the dispute unilaterally, her mother determined to stop the fight and, despite warning cries from the onlookers, succeeded with the aid of a long wooden clothes prop. The two men returned next day to apologise.

The vast quantities of stone aggregate required for airfield construction were brought in by a fleet of lorries operated by a company based in Southend. Young Nancy Moore, who was running the garage in Knodishall after the early death of her father, remembers the endless task of filling their fuel tanks by means of an old hand-operated overhead pump that delivered only half a gallon per cycle. One or two of the lorry drivers discovered it was possible to obtain multiple receipts, and thus multiple payments, for a single load by making several passes across the airfield without tipping, leaving on each occasion by an un-gated exit. Despite such unpatriotic behaviour the base was completed within twelve months and became operational in October 1943, not before some battle-damaged B-17s had already used a completed runway for an emergency landing earlier that summer, Leiston being the airfield closest to the North Sea coast.

The first units to arrive at the base were those of the 358th Fighter Group equipped with P-47 Thunderbolt fighters but, as these lacked the necessary range to escort bombers into Germany, they were transferred south in January 1944 for operations over France. The next day Station 373 became home to the Mustangs of the 357th Fighter Group. Attached as a support unit with the 357th was the 1076th Signal Company, which listed on its strength Sgt. Ed Rosenthal 39842293.

Atlantic Crossing

After leaving the induction camp in Reno, Edwin had moved through some fourteen other training camps in the western and southern states learning to send and receive Morse code at forty words per minute together with the various other procedures relevant to military signalling. But by the late summer of 1943, with his training largely completed and the time approaching for transfer overseas, his skills as a newspaperman were noted and given precedence over his value as a signaller: he was marked for a role as a public relations correspondent.

On 17 October he wrote from the Army Air Base at Dyersburg, Tennessee to his younger brother Bob at home on Long Island, now married with the first of three sons. The letter remarks on the erosion of personal morality affecting soldiers after a few months within the institutionalised environment of the army, and illustrates the fact with the story of his own recent entanglement with alcohol and a divorced Tennessee girl called Alene. This, while reading like the outline for a short story, seems shot through with a combination of fantasy – probably arising from all-male army society – and envy for the secured life of the married man, this betrayed by a desire to impress his younger brother with an exaggerated account of what he is missing. He goes on to admit having lost interest in baseball, a previous passion, which, particularly in the case of a sports writer, might be seen as indicative of preoccupation with the immediate prospect of transfer to a war zone rather than with the amorous opportunities provided by army life. Whatever the barrack-room psychology, the letter is clearly from the hand of a man pensive and nervous on the eve of departure to war.

That departure came the following month with the 1076th Signal Company being called to New York for embarkation on the *Queen Mary*. Ed was able to spend his last night in the United States at home with his family in Woodmere. It may have been on that night that he and his father achieved the resolution of their differences which Ed refers to in correspondence after Sig's death the following May; the possibility of a son's death overseas may have been the necessary catalyst.

Ed was to make the Atlantic crossing on the *Queen Mary* many times during the post-war years when the ship had returned to her intended role as a luxury liner, but on this, his maiden voyage, the *Queen Mary* was carrying 15,000 troops in cramped conditions rather than 2,000 well-heeled civilians travelling in spacious comfort. She and her sister ship the *Queen Elizabeth* made these dangerous crossings without escort, their speed of thirty knots combined with a constantly zig-zagging course providing protection from the U-boat packs. Many GIs assumed such impressive machinery must be American and could not understand why American ships should be named after English monarchs.

On docking in the Clyde the troops entrained for their various destinations. Their first views of Britain as seen from the train windows invariably engendered surprise. Surprise at its verdant scenery, even in winter, at the smallness of the roads, of the cars and of the train itself. Surprise at the neat tidiness of the villages uncluttered by billboards, and surprise moving to shock at the gaping ruins of fresh bomb damage punctuating the dismal-looking streets of the towns and cities. To avoid assisting enemy map-reading in the event of invasion, road signs had been removed, as had nameplates from the railway stations; many Americans thought when ordered from the train that they had arrived at a town called Hovis. A more personal surprise on those trains equipped with corridors and toilets was the hard, shiny toilet paper more akin to greaseproof paper than to soft American tissue.

Over Here

The way they walked, the way they talked! They always walked in great groups and took up half the road; they weren't showy, they were just jolly big physical fellows … And they were always talking and they all seemed to be having fun … They were just larger than life. They could have come from outer space, there was that much difference.

Despite official silence the people of Leiston and the surrounding villages knew it was the Americans who would be coming to the new airfield. Units of the 8th Army Air Force had been arriving in East Anglia at an increasing pace over the twelve months since tentative operations had begun in the late summer of 1942. Through parts of Suffolk and Norfolk it seemed as if every other parish had an airfield under construction and it was no secret they were for the Yanks. The Germans also knew, and on the arrival of the Americans at Leiston their propagandist announcer Lord Haw-Haw, with only minimally incorrect geography, broadcast a message welcoming them to Yoxford. Thus arose the 357th's official nickname of 'The Yoxford Boys'. The locals were not sure what to expect, as for most their only exposure to matters American had been vicariously by way of Hollywood and the Leiston Picture House. In that less cynical age some no doubt mistook image for reality and were anticipating plane-loads of Clark Gables descending (Clark Gable did actually serve with the 8th Air Force at Polebrook, Cambridgeshire as a B-17 gunner although primarily for publicity purposes).

Usually the first sighting of the new allies was of unusually relaxed-looking young men hurtling around the lanes surrounding the base in open Jeeps, unusual in an age of few cars and scarce petrol. Dependent on age and gender the observer on foot or bicycle would be greeted with ebullient passing cries of 'Howdy Pop!' or 'Hiya kids!', 'Howdy Ma'am' or 'Hello Honey!' They might even be offered a lift. Should the men be in air force uniform with shoes and buttons shining, trousers pressed and stylish caps at a jaunty angle with the driver chewing a cigar, then those anticipating Hollywood might not have been too disappointed. It was this exuberant, easygoing attitude to life in the military, and to life in general, that so marked the Yanks apart. Born in the land of opportunity and proud of that country and its cause, the Americans possessed a characteristic vitality virtually absent from wartime Britain.

The slang-ridden drawl mirrored the casual attitude of the GI as did his walk, a slouching role in comfortable cotton clothes and rubber-soled boots contrasting to the noisy clatter and stiff carriage of British troops in their rough wool serge and leather. They paid only minimal attention to officers and to military etiquette in general, throwing, to British eyes, the sloppy 'long way up-short way down' US salute as opposed to the crisp reverse version of the British forces. They constantly chewed gum, could be seen eating in the street and even sitting on the pavement in the towns. They paid equally little regard to rules, often offering civilians – particularly pretty ones – lifts in military vehicles and allowed inquisitive schoolboys into security areas on the base. They were relaxed and friendly, with an open breeziness foreign to British reserve. They also possessed a spontaneous generosity of spirit that would have come as a surprise to the guarded suspicions of any rural population, but which came especially so to the shy and reticent people of Suffolk.

Any perceived sloppiness in approach to military behaviour and bearing was in contrast to the smartness of the lightweight tailored uniforms which, worn with shoes as opposed to boots, and decorated with medals and ribbons for nothing more than service overseas, could give even a private the appearance of an officer. The average American male was generally larger in physique with better teeth than the less well-fed British man and his attention to personal hygiene was also usually superior. Although a tendency toward the use of aftershave and deodorant and to the wearing of rings, wrist-watches and neck-chains brought accusations of effeminacy from British troops, the reality was that, as far as British girls were concerned, the American could not help but be seen as the better prize. Particularly as he enjoyed the advantage of relative affluence, US service pay being some four to five times higher than for equivalent rank in the British forces. As this was paid monthly to GIs rather than weekly as for the British, the Americans periodically found their hip pockets bulging with money that encouraged celebration and generous hospitality off-base.

Apart from desirable men the American bases were also a source of supply for commodities long-missing or else severely rationed in Britain. Sweets, chocolate, tinned fruit, meat, coffee, cheese, sugar; all could come the way of a favoured young woman and her family. And while that much-sought prize, nylon stockings, were not usually held in the base stores, they could be posted from the US by relatives or friends who were sometimes briefed to be careful not to arouse the suspicions of stateside partners. Joyce Leek received hers, beautiful variants decorated with black butterflies, interleaved within the pages of a rolled-up copy of the *Kansas City Courier* mailed by the mother of her GI friend Jeff. A bikini later arrived the same way.

Joyce had married Bill Leek from Hill Farm in 1942 but, having been unable to find an affordable home of their own, they were still living separately with their respective parents when the Americans arrived. Helping her mother to man the crossing gates adjacent to the southern end of the airfield, Joyce could not help but meet the Yanks who themselves could not help but chat up an attractive young woman, married or not. This could bring its own dangers, not because Jeff ever made an un-gentlemanly suggestion, or because Bill was violently jealous, but because trains were frequent. On a breezy morning when Joyce's mother was busy with the washing she took in from some of the men on the base, Joyce had been left in charge of the gates. Distracted by saucy repartee swapped with the driver of an air force Jeep, Joyce failed to hear the warning 'train approaching' bell in the wind and was startled by the sudden, frantic whistling of a locomotive approaching at speed. With a yelled 'Goddamn!' the American lurched off the crossing a split-second before the train roared through, splintering the heavy timber gates. Joyce's father had to travel to Norwich to explain the circumstances.

Perhaps spurred by the circumstances of this accident, or by the arrival of the elegant nylons and skimpy bikini, Joyce's mother proffered the timeless warning that her daughter should be careful because 'they are all after the same thing dear!' Joyce replied 'Yes, I know. But it's how they go after it what makes the difference!' And that, despite the looks, the money and the food, was the crux of the matter. American society with its free mingling of the sexes at high school, the drugstore and college, had better trained its young men in the courtship of women. Joyce put a word to it – 'They were, above all else, *attentive.*' The local lad might buy his girl a shandy and a packet of crisps in the pub, and then ignore her while he talked or played darts with his mates. The American would flatter, listen, open a door or offer a chair, all with an infectious air of light-hearted good humour that would make a girl feel centre-stage and set her heart reeling. This, combined with the material advantages of knowing a GI – not least privileged access to the base dances – meant there really was no competition from the local men, most of whom were away at war in any case. As Joyce put it 'The Yanks took the place by storm!'

Annie

At Mill House the joy and relief of Jack Thorpe's sudden return from the Far East was prelude to an intensification of his romance with Anne Jordan. After two weeks leave Jack was ordered to HMS *Defiance*, the naval training station at Devonport, to prepare for re-allocation to the destroyer fleet. Letters to and from Anne passed back and forth on an almost daily basis containing no more than expressions of mutual love, although Jack's occasionally recorded interruptions to his writing by German raids on Plymouth, large exclamation marks indicating the noise of the anti-aircraft guns.

Infrequently through that summer and autumn a few days leave from Devonport would coincide with an off-duty weekend for Hilda and Anne at the factory in St Albans allowing the three to gather at Mill House. They got on famously. Each was of a free-spirited, rebellious nature tempered by an irreverent sense of humour and a love of socialising. The war was slowly loosening the stifling corset of formal propriety that had previously governed British society. It was a new sort of war that put civilians on the frontline and there had been too much death, too much loss and pain too close to home for the old order not to be questioned; priorities were being reassessed, which suited the threesome well enough.

In name and practice Florrie was responsible for the domestic management of the front half of Mill House. But in the face of her dominating mother-in-law any temporarily-increased weight of authority she might have enjoyed as the mother of two young children had faded with their maturity and she had resumed a quiet obeisance. At only four foot ten inches tall and seven stone she was small and timid, often lacking the confidence even to foray out to Mrs Moore's shop on the other side of the Common; yet her gentle nature and tiny size engendered affection in all who discovered her. Meanwhile Alice, now in her seventies, had lost none of her steel and still exercised an overbearing supervision of her son's household. Alice's home in the rear half of Mill House, where she lived with Charlie in a time-warp of candlelight, rag-rugs and fat bacon, connected internally with the front half through a long, unlit corridor that could seem to Florrie like a dark portal to an earlier age. Several times each day its echoing plain-boarded floor would sound a warning as Alice approached in her clumpy black shoes and thick brown stockings, sending Florrie's heart sinking. This imbalance of female power in Mill House did not go unobserved and, whereas to Hilda it had always been the way of things, to newcomer Anne it was an injustice she saw as nothing less than her duty to challenge.

She began with the washing. Alice was nothing if not a traditionalist and the whole of each Monday was devoted to the household's laundry. Beds were stripped, clothes, tablecloths, tea-towels and antimacassars collected up by the armful and, with curt instructions from Granny Alice not to let loose ends trail on the floor, lugged heavily to the rear scullery where Charlie would have had the fire going under the big copper since before the sun was up. Each category of washing would in turn be dumped into the boiling water, stirred about with giant wooden tongs and then lifted out item by item to drain in the scullery sink in what Alice considered to be a sterilizing pre-wash. The process was then repeated but with the addition of soap-powder to the water and hand-rubbing on a washboard, followed by two rinsings in clean water before everything was squeezed through the rollers of a massive cast-iron Victorian mangle which Florrie could turn only by throwing her whole body-weight against the cranked handle.

By mid-morning the mangle would have produced a damp hillock of heavy, creased linen which was then hauled out to the yard, Alice and Florrie on either side of the wicker basket, and fastened to the line with the split wooden pegs purchased from the gypsies. If it should be a bright windy day, ironing with the heavy flat irons kept sitting atop Alice's black-leaded range could begin in the afternoon, but more often this operation would stretch into the following morning. By Monday evening, finally dismissed, Florrie's small hands would be red-raw and her nose running from the combination of steam and wet linen. Exhausted, she would sink briefly onto the old hardback chair in her own kitchen for a few moments respite, praying that there was enough cold meat left for George's supper.

Annie had witnessed this procedure once on the Monday of a long weekend at Mill House and on the next occasion she found herself in Knodishall on a washday she was determined to introduce some exhaustion-reducing efficiency. It was September 1942 and it seemed increasingly on the cards that Florrie might soon be her mother-in-law. This did not go down tremendously well with Alice who was confident that, with a little more patience, her grandson could do a good deal better than marry a domestic turned factory worker from the west of Ireland. Whatever Jack's quota of patience it was not something Annie had in surplus when she volunteered to take over the ageing Alice's wash duties this Monday morning and brushed aside the vigorous protestation. Granny Alice had finally met her match.

Annie confidently took charge, dispensing with the time-consuming pre-wash routine and rejecting the washboard in favour of a vigorous paddling with the tongs followed by one rinse instead of two. She then threw herself into a wild winding of the mangle handle, shouting to Florrie to mind her fingers as feeding the linen into the rollers Florrie rushed to keep pace. Alice stood in the doorway through to her kitchen harrumphing throughout, but by 9.30am everything was pegged and blowing in the wind. At which point Alice, hands on pinafored hips and wearing a murderous expression, marched up and down the lines of sheets like an inspecting officer searching for an undone button. Now and then she pulled a sheet corner to her nose for a good smell but all was sweetly clean until, on turning the final corner there, across the corner of a pillowcase, was a ragged black line looking very much like a soot mark. 'Hmmm!' exhaled Alice loudly, pointing at the pillowcase and glaring victoriously toward Annie, who wasn't looking at all but was pursuing Hilda into the back garden with threats of bodily harm. A fortnight later a grateful Florrie reported to Hilda that Alice had, without any comment, adopted the new regime, although her opinion of Anne did not seem to have been enhanced.

Whatever Alice's feelings, everybody else loved Annie. To Hilda she was best mate; Florrie thought her a breath of fresh air; George quietly conceded she was 'alright' which, for a Suffolk man, was the pinnacle of praise; and Jack was in love with her. Charlie wisely kept his own counsel but was, as ever, warm and welcoming. Rarely during the winter of 1942–43 a twenty-four-hour leave enabled Jack to catch the train up from Plymouth to spend a few brief hours with Anne in St Albans. On those occasions Hilda and Agnes would thoughtfully be elsewhere, leaving the lovers to kiss and cuddle on the worn sofa at 130 Waverley Road. In the spring the memory of those intimate winter afternoons spent by the light of the gas fire became the stuff of sustenance for Jack who, in April, was posted to the hard grey steel of the 'M'-class destroyer HMS *Mahratta*, just commissioned and 'working up' in northern waters off Scapa Flow.

The *Mahratta* was to spend most of her life escorting the Arctic convoys from their assembly point at Loch Ewe in the west of Scotland around the North Cape of Norway to the Russian Arctic port of Murmansk in the Barents Sea. She was delayed in taking up this duty during her first operational summer, as the Russian convoys had been suspended until the autumn. Escort priority had been decided in favour of the Atlantic convoys which were continuing to suffer heavy losses from the U-boats and which were also threatened by the potential break-out to the Atlantic of the German battleships *Tirpitz*, *Scharnhorst* and *Lutzow* lurking in the Norwegian fiords. The other factor in deciding on a summer curtailment was that the long hours of daylight and better weather greatly increased the exposure of the slow-moving convoys to air attack from Luftwaffe forces based in occupied Norway.

The *Mahratta*, however, stayed in northern waters and in July and August made her first high-speed runs to Russia carrying supplies and personnel to Murmansk. With a top speed of almost forty knots she was capable of keeping herself out of most trouble. She was also involved in diversionary operations feinting an invasion of Norway; this aimed at ensuring continuing German commitment in northern Europe away from the Sicilian landings. After five months in the north she was ordered south to Biscay in September to assist with the escort of Royal Navy carriers returning from the Mediterranean to Britain for repairs, and on 10 October 1943 she arrived at Plymouth for an overhaul, some six months after Jack had last spoken to Anne.

He was not at liberty to tell her much about where he had been or what he had been doing, except in general terms, which were enough to impress upon them both that life was far too risky to be put on hold and that they should get married at the very first opportunity. Opportunity was very much the problem because the *Mahratta* was about to return to the distant Arctic for winter escort duties in what was one of the most dangerous and uncomfortable theatres of operation of the whole war.

North to Murmansk

Until June 1941 Hitler and Stalin, though not exactly allies, were cooperating under the non-aggression pact signed secretly by Molotov and Ribbentrop in August 1939. They had shared out Poland between them and Russia had seized the Baltic States and Finland without German interference. Choosing to be deaf to plentiful warnings of the coming storm, Stalin continued to sanction exports of fuel and grain to Germany right up to 22 June when at 3am Hitler launched his forces in Operation Barbarossa, an eastward *blitzkrieg* toward Moscow and the oilfields of the Caucasus.

Suddenly Britain no longer stood alone against Nazi Germany; on its side was the whole vast extent of the Soviet empire, rich in territory, natural resources and manpower, though poor in modern technology and manufacturing capacity. On the evening of 22 June Churchill broadcast a message pledging all possible support to Germany's new enemy. No warm cooperation of comrades-in-arms followed. Rather, Stalin imperiously demanded, almost from the day of invasion, that a second front be opened immediately and that war materiel be delivered regularly and in quantity. The first demand was an impossibility at the time but Churchill was anxious to help with the second, knowing that it was important to keep Stalin on-side. Recognising him for the ruthless, pragmatic dictator that he was, Churchill realised Stalin was quite capable of agreeing a separate peace with the Nazis should it be to his advantage, a move which would profoundly alter the outcome of the war.

At the time, with the Luftwaffe dominant over the Mediterranean, there were only three routes to get supplies to Russia: the long haul through to the Pacific in the east, the southern route around the Cape to the Persian Gulf, and the Arctic route around the North Cape of German-occupied Norway. The last was the shortest and most direct but also the most difficult and certainly the most dangerous. At the Admiralty, the First Sea Lord, Sir Dudley Pound, thought the proposition 'most unsound in every way'. If the Arctic weather were not threat enough, enemy aircraft and surface ships based in Norway, combined with the submarine threat, 'loaded the dice against us in every direction'. And in any event the Navy was already being hard-pressed on all fronts: in the East, in the Mediterranean and particularly in the Atlantic, where the battle to keep Britain herself supplied was reaching a crescendo in the teeth of increasing U-boat attacks.

Yet those who felt political expediency should not be allowed to dictate military strategy were overruled. Churchill was famous, per-haps notorious, for pugnacious determination. Difficulties were to be overcome, the Arctic convoys would proceed. After a small explora-tory run to north Russia in August the first of the convoys proper sailed north-east from Iceland on 28 September 1941, its destination the White Sea port of Archangel, its loading including twenty tanks and nearly 200 fighter aircraft.

As Archangel was ice-bound for much of the year, most subsequent convoys were obliged to terminate at the bleak and poorly-devel-oped port of Murmansk on the Barents Sea, barely twenty-five miles from the front-line with German-occupied Norway. Nevertheless the first few convoys got through relatively unscathed that autumn, largely unnoticed by the Germans who were preoccupied with anticipation of a British invasion of Norway. The situation was not to last. In the New Year the Russians counterattacked on the Eastern Front and Hitler determined to use all available forces to prevent their re-supply. Arctic geography was on his side: winter ice pushed the Allied convoys toward the Norwegian coast to within range of the Luftwaffe's dive-bombers; the heavily stratified waters off that coast – caused by admixture of the declining Gulf Stream with the denser seas of the Arctic – diminished the anti-submarine capabilities of the escorting warships by confusing their ASDIC sonar systems, and the natural bastion of the deep fiords gave protection to the powerful surface ships he relocated to Norway. But his greatest ally was the weather.

From the day a convoy began to form up in the Minch outside Loch Ewe it was liable to be raked by gales and storms that made maintaining position difficult and, if sufficiently violent, could threaten the survival of the heavily-laden ships, many of which were long past their best. Neither were warships immune from serious damage: armour plating could be peeled from forward gun turrets when plunging bows were buried under walls of 'green' water crashing over the vessel. But it was as the merchantmen climbed into the higher latitudes and narrowing longitudes, plugging north at a steady eight knots, that difficulties became acute. The cold reached an intensity that caused winches, guns and gun turrets to seize solid and froze sea-spray into icy shrapnel that clattered across the decks. The grey seas concealed submerged 'growler' icebergs, or were jammed with pack ice, either of which could spring the thin hulls of merchantmen and warships alike. Frequently the lowering, leaden skies enveloped a convoy in squally blizzards of snow and sleet which reduced visibility to zero but, far worse, drove the freezing spray and spume over icebound decks and superstructures sheathing them in steadily accreting layers of ice that had to be constantly chipped away else the ship capsize with the top-heavy weight.

For those coming off a long watch or ice-clearing duty little solace was available below the decks of a vessel plunging and rolling through heavy seas. The ships enjoyed no special preparation for Arctic duty: as one Navy officer remarked 'when we moved up from the Med. all we could do was to put on a vest and shut the windows.' Hard angles and blunt edges threatened to batter bodies not tightly hugging supports. Steel bulkheads ran with condensation, decks and galley-ways with seawater. Eating, like movement, could be a challenge, sometimes resolved by emptying tins of soup into a steel bucket to be heated with a blow torch and passed around the mess. Yet such stormy weather could be welcome for, as with fog and mist, it concealed a convoy from the reconnaissance planes and dive-bombers that inevitably appeared once visibility improved.

The U-boats were not so weather-dependent. Though reliant on reconnaissance aircraft for precise information as to a convoy's whereabouts, they would lay in wait athwart the main routes, particularly where these funnelled together to round the North Cape on the approach to Murmansk. Under cover of darkness a U-boat could approach a convoy on the surface at seventeen knots without triggering the sonar detection of the escorting warships. It would then submerge before resurfacing to periscope depth within the lines of ships where, with a multitude of slow-moving targets, its torpedoes were likely to send thousands of tons of tanks, planes, guns and all the other requisites of war to the seabed. Together with the ships' crews who, if not incinerated or dismembered by the blast, could not live for more than a few minutes in the freezing seas.

A safe arrival in Murmansk provided only limited relief. The heavily-bombed harbour of rotting timber wharves and minimal offloading facilities offered few useable berths, forcing loaded ships awaiting their turn to ride at anchor, often for weeks, while all the time exposed to constant raids from the nearest German airfield in Norway, a mere fifteen minutes flying time distant. Things were no better ashore where there was a dismal absence of facilities for relaxation or recreation. Nor did the Russians seem at all pleased by the arrival of the supplies and equipment delivered at such huge cost. Any survivor of a traumatic passage north who might have anticipated sympathy or gratitude, or just friendly cooperation, quickly realised his mistake. To the contrary, within Russian officialdom a tendency to surly, suspicious truculence seemed to mirror Stalin's own uncompromising attitude which combined demands for evermore convoys with complaints regarding supplies already received, and a refusal to recognise any of the hazardous logistics involved in their delivery. At the personal level any prospect of easy cooperation between allies was smothered by a sour paranoia engendered by the presence of the political commissars embedded throughout the Russian administration. These watchful 'thought police' inevitably attended even the most insignificant exchanges.

Particularly demoralising for the seamen who had fought through these deliveries at such huge risk was the sight of the offloaded equipment left to rust on the docksides, often still there when they returned on a subsequent convoys months later. The fact that such wasted weaponry was frequently more up-to-date than that currently in use by British forces, and was sorely needed in other theatres of war, increased their disillusionment. Russian shortcomings were also evident in a failure to provide the level of surface escort and air cover which Churchill had hoped his ally might undertake in the Barents Sea approaches to Murmansk. Those few Russian units which were deployed did their best, often with great gallantry, but Stalin, pointedly ignorant of the situation at sea, felt under no obligation to assist. In any event the Royal Navy noted that, while Russian ice-breaking technique in the White Sea was excellent, the fleet work of their navy was hopeless (perhaps not surprising given that the one nation occupied a small island while the other held the world's greatest land mass).

Russian guards, often large women, impeded personnel movements ashore by insisting on the production of visas and passes and miscellaneous paperwork which in most cases did not exist (situations could sometimes be resolved by the production of an adequate amount of the local currency – cigarettes and chocolate). Russian hospital facilities were denied to wounded seamen and, when a field hospital unit was delivered to overcome this particular difficulty, the Russians refused to accept it: it was eventually installed aboard a British ship. Any unusually friendly Russian encountered was more than likely a member of the NKVD, the secret police, intent on gathering information.

Yet, away from all the suspicious paranoia of Russian officialdom, the ordinary citizens were friendly enough, if cautiously so given the constant surveillance. Bob Townshend was 2nd Radio Officer on the merchantman *Hope Ranger* and recalls that the form in the street was to stand on a corner discreetly displaying a handful of cigarettes. These would be gently removed by the first passer-by who, with a quick surreptitious smile, would replace them with a wad of grimy rouble notes that could be exchanged for vodka and food at the rough and ready International Sailors' Club.

Living conditions for the civilian population were dire. Roughly two-thirds of the town had been destroyed by German bombing, which was ongoing, and those buildings still habitable were without glass or any services in winter weather conditions which, in that latitude, are extremely severe. Near starvation resulted in pilfering from ships and docksides when opportunity arose, despite the risk of falling foul of summary Soviet justice. A dock-worker caught with a purloined jar of jam was beaten to death; another found with a pair of long-johns pulled from a split bale aboard the merchantman *Henry Villard* was shot on the spot.

On balance there was very little reason for seamen to go ashore except perhaps to get the feel of ground under their feet and take some land-based exercise, which was why Lieutenant-Commander Gower of the destroyer HMS *Swift* took his crew onto a jetty for a 'tug o' war' match, stokers v. seamen. A suitable length of stout rope was found, a mark was made on the jetty between the two teams, two ribbons were attached to the rope either side of the mark and the match began, much intriguing a group of baffled Russians. It was best of three and eventually the stokers won, at which point a uniformed Russian officer approached Gower from behind and, tapping him on the shoulder, said quietly to his ear, 'Look, if you need to break that rope it would be much easier to cut it.'

After a slow start the Germans had, by the spring of 1942, largely got the measure of the Arctic convoys and despite vigorous defending by the escorts, losses mounted. The Admiralty, realising that the more or less permanent daylight of the Arctic summer would greatly increase the exposure of the convoys to both spotter and attack aircraft, pressed Churchill for a suspension until the autumn. But the Prime Minister insisted: whatever the risk the flow of arms to the Eastern Front must continue. Stalin was advancing, momentum must not be lost. As with his instruction to the defenders of Hong Kong to fight to the last man, Churchill did not baulk at the sacrifice of forces where he deemed it necessary to the bigger picture. But the Admiralty was right, the Arctic summer of 1942 was bloody.

The lowest point came in July with the devastation of convoy PQ17 which on 4 July received orders from the Sir Dudley Pound in London to scatter for fear that the German battleship *Tirpitz* was about to engage. The escorting warships withdrew at speed expecting a sea-battle, but the *Tirpitz* failed to appear. The awful realisation dawned that the dispersed, unprotected merchant ships had been abandoned to be hunted down one by one by the U-boats and dive-bombers. Of the 36 that had sailed north 24 were eventually sunk with the loss of over 400 tanks, 200 planes, thousands of vehicles and a 100,000 tons of munitions. A bigger loss, or perhaps one of longer-lasting significance, was of such trust as the Merchant Navy had held in its fighting counterpart. Particularly damaged was American respect for the Royal Navy for although 153 merchant seaman died on PQ17 the ill-conceived order 'Convoy is to scatter' meant that not one Navy sailor died in their defence.

The convoys continued through the following winter season until their suspension for the summer beginning, despite Stalin's protests, in March 1943 when all available warships were committed to the climactic weeks in the Battle of the Atlantic. By the time the *Mahratta* took up escort duties with the resumed convoys in late October the situation had changed significantly. The crisis in the Atlantic had passed: Allied troops had invaded Italy and were fighting towards Rome; the Germans were in serious trouble in Russia; and Allied military planners were turning their thoughts towards the invasion of mainland Europe. The tide had turned against Hitler and the Arctic convoys moved up a gear. By now it had been realised that continuous air cover was essential for convoy protection and the 'escort' carrier, a smaller version of a full-scale aircraft carrier, had been designed to provide it. Initially these were converted merchant ships fitted with a flight deck and equipped with up to thirty warplanes including the tough new American Wildcat. Accompanying warship escorts were increased in size and number with enhanced anti-aircraft and anti-submarine capabilities. Confidence was building: as Jack wrote in a letter to Anne: 'if we keep winning this lot should soon be over.'

Friends and Family

Mail from loved ones, hot cocoa and black humour formed a large part of the sustenance of sailors. Jack wrote to Anne daily when his duties allowed and Anne reciprocated, after all they had a wedding to plan, but planning, with the groom unreachable for long periods on the Arctic seas, was difficult. Jack, concerned primarily with surviving for long enough to get to the wedding, was obliged to leave it all to Anne. He did ask a few shipmates if they would like to be guests at the marriage but all apologetically admitted that their first priority on receiving leave in England would be to rush to their own families. Anxious to have everything ready for the moment when leave sufficient for a wedding did materialise, Anne had organised a wedding cake to be ready for mid-November, but with the *Mahratta* fully occupied in the Arctic she began to worry that it might dry out before anyone had a chance to eat it. She wrote to Jack that he better hurry back and get on with it. Fortuitously the *Mahratta* was ordered to escort the returning convoy RA54B back to Loch Ewe where she arrived on 9 December. Shortly afterwards Jack was on a train on his way home to Suffolk where, on 16 December 1943 at the Catholic church in Leiston, Father William Jolly presided over his marriage to Anne Jordan.

The reception was at Mill House and those able to be present more than enjoyed the occasion, though at such short notice it had been difficult to arrange for any surfeit of food and drink. Nevertheless the cake had taken no harm, friends and neighbours had chipped in generously, and Charlie had provided a dozen bottles of his notorious parsnip wine. Alice had sensed that her duty lay with the catering and, with Florrie as labourer, had spent two solid days baking. But by mid-evening Hilda and Agnes had decided that with the preponderance of old folk who had by now reverted to drinking tea, the party was becoming just a tad quiet so they slipped out unobtrusively to The Butcher's Arms next door for a Saturday night drink.

Charlie Ablett, the landlord, was not known for his good humour nor for any great sociability. He was quite likely, on a particularly grumpy day, to hang his tea-towel over the pumps and close early, shunting out the complaining drinkers to allow him to attend to the pigs he kept behind the pub. Saturday nights were usually salvaged by there being sufficient clientele at the bar to enable the dour weight of his presence to be overwhelmed by alcoholically-charged goodwill. Hilda bought Agnes and herself double gins and orange and immediately threw herself into the conversational melee as she always did but, after a moment or two, she realised that Agnes was uncharacteristically quiet. Following her friend's fixed gaze she saw at the end of the bar the tall, undisputedly handsome figure of Eric Goodwin, home on leave and looking particularly fine this night in the dark blue uniform of the Royal Marines. Twenty-four year-old Agnes was transfixed: 'Who is that?' she whispered breathlessly to Hilda. 'Oh him?' replied Hilda dismissively 'He's just a local boy. Come on, I'll introduce you.'

There was one immediate family member unable to attend the celebration. Jack's Uncle Clifford had got himself into some difficulty. Things had already gone badly wrong for Clifford before the war when his loyal and unassuming wife, Dorothy, had died in tragic circumstances. If Florrie's role as daughter-in-law to Alice was difficult, Dorothy's, as wife to the favourite son, had been impossible. Despite having two young children, her husband was rarely with her. He left early to take his breakfast with his parents at Mill House, spent his day there helping Charlie and returned only after his evening meal. His simple mind, easily influenced, provided fallow ground to accommodate his mother's jealous coolness towards his wife. He did at least sleep in his own marital bed but it was from there the problem stemmed. However it was that he came upon the idea, when Dorothy became pregnant with a third child, Clifford decided that another mouth to feed represented an unacceptable burden, and so took matters into his own hands, literally. Dorothy, with the child aborted, died of the subsequent infection. The other children went to her mother in Ipswich and Clifford returned permanently to his mother's fold.

Wifeless, Clifford's sexuality simmered dangerously unreleased until, with the emotional and physical upheaval of the war, as the old parameters of rural society cracked and shifted, it seeped to the surface in the form of obscene letters addressed to various married women in the village. Several were sent to Alf Moore's wife, aunt to Hilda's friend Nancy. After the first one arrived Alf went to the police station in Leiston and an investigation was launched into the sordid business. At first the finger fell on Eric's brother-in-law, little Jimmy Atkins, owner of the Alsatian that had survived 'Moody's Hole'. Jimmy had about an acre of land on a distant edge of the Common, high-fenced with chicken wire and guarded by the Alsatian. Within it he had constructed a rusty shanty town of corrugated tin huts to accommodate his pigs. Police thinking was that as he spent far more time in there than was required to husband the pigs, he might be up to no good. Alf was apoplectic with rage and threatened to kill Jimmy, before hand-writing analysis acquitted Jimmy and eventually convicted Clifford, sending him for a term in Norwich gaol. Which is where he was on the day of Jack's wedding.

Hilda and Agnes collected Clifford on his release. It seemed that, despite all the business of the investigation and trial, he had failed to grasp that he had done anything particularly out of the ordinary for which remorse might be due. He described the food he had been given, and the activities he had been provided with, as if he had been sent on a holiday rather than a penance, concluding with the observation that it had been 'lovely and warm in there'. The penance was served by the family at home, obliged to endure the shame, although those who knew Clifford realised his family could hardly be held accountable. For her part Alice had coped by observing a complete denial, inwardly and outwardly, refusing to acknowledge the matter even to Charlie.

Arctic Tragedy

Obliged to return to his ship over Christmas, Jack managed to get back to Anne for a weekend in the New Year before the *Mahratta* resumed escort duties in mid-January helping to shepherd convoy JW56B to Murmansk and bringing RA56 back. He continued to write daily when he could, now able to sign off letters crammed with sweet nothings 'your loving husband'. They passed swiftly past the censor, carrying no news, only the affectionate outpourings of a besotted lover missing his new wife and impatient for hostilities to end so they might be together forever. But there was still a long way to go before Hitler was defeated and what Jack, expressing hopes to Anne that it might soon be over, could not know as a mere Able Seaman was the latest development in German strategy.

The U-boats had lost the Battle of the Atlantic due to improved Allied air cover and anti-submarine techniques coupled with the cracking of the Enigma code which had allowed the interception of their communications. Admiral Donitz, their commander-in-chief, now decided to concentrate his fleet in the Arctic in a desperate effort to cut off supplies to the advancing Red Army. Well aware that the sinking of just one freighter heavily loaded with tanks and munitions was the equivalent, in materiel destroyed, of a significant land-based victory, Donitz determined that insofar as he was able to effect it, such supplies to the Russians would get no further east than the bed of the Barents Sea. To help him he now had at his disposal the new T-5 'Gnat' acoustic torpedo which homed in on wake and propeller noise and which therefore made the targeting of fast-moving warships a more viable proposition.

The next convoy north was a big one, designed to push as much through to the Eastern Front as possible before the requirements of the D-Day invasion obliged a temporary halt. JW 57 left Loch Ewe on 20 February 1944 with some fifty merchant ships and a correspondingly powerful ocean escort that included the escort carrier HMS *Chaser*, the anti-aircraft cruiser HMS *Black Prince*, three further cruisers and thirteen destroyers including the *Mahratta*. An innovation was the equipping of the *Chaser's* aircraft with searchlights for night-time anti-submarine operations. Four days into the voyage the first U-boats appeared, homed in by reconnaissance aircraft. The destroyer HMS *Keppel* sank one and the next day, the 25th, a Catalina flying boat operating at extreme range from the Shetlands sank another. With the destroyers towing dummy targets of metal scrap to decoy the 'Gnats' the convoy plodded on toward the North Cape.

That night the defensive dispositions signalled from Vice-Admiral Glennie on board *Black Prince* caused some raised eyebrows amongst one or two of the destroyer officers now on Arctic convoy after long experience in the Atlantic. Weather conditions were poor, with zero visibility and a rough sea favouring the undetected surface approach of submarines, but to screen the rear of the convoy, the most likely quarter for attack, Glennie positioned only two destroyers, the *Mahratta* and the *Impulsive*. The destroyer men had great faith in the hugely-experienced leadership of their Captain of Destroyers, Ian Campbell in HMS *Milne*, but were sometimes less sanguine about the judgement of more distant admirals. On this occasion their doubts were well-founded.

Just before 9pm the radio rooms in the warships picked up a message to the flagship *Black Prince* from Lieutenant-Commander Drought in command of the *Mahratta*: 'Hit by torpedo aft, am stopped'. The voice was calm and measured. A few minutes later a second message came through in more anguished tones over a terrible background noise of shouting and confusion: 'Hit amidships by second torpedo.' And then: 'We are abandoning ship. We cannot last much longer.' Kapitanleutnant Nordheimer in *U-990* had successfully fired first a 'Gnat' and then a conventional torpedo at the destroyer which was now sinking fast. In the darkness those not killed or incapacitated by the blasts were jumping into the icy blackness of the sea where they knew their life expectancy was no more than five minutes. Eighteen-year-old seaman Jack Humble fought his way up to the deck through a tangle of blast debris to find men shouting for wives and mothers as they went into the water. Swept overboard he was sucked down by the sinking ship but then surfaced on a sea covered with the silent bodies of dead sailors. Doused in heavy fuel oil, which may have saved him, he was dragged aboard the *Impulsive* by his hair fifteen minutes later, one of only seventeen survivors from a crew of 240. Drought went down with his ship. Lieutenant-Commander Gower, in command of the nearby *Swift*, heard his final message. He had been with him at Dartmouth and remembers him as 'a good little hockey player'. Of the newly-married Jack Thorpe there was no trace.

The convoy reached Russia without further loss of warships or merchant vessels and, having cost only one ship despite a concentrated U-boat presence, was considered a great success. News of the *Mahratta's* loss was withheld until 18 March. When it came there might have been those at Scott's Shipyard on the Clyde who were not completely surprised. Her keel had been laid down in the yard in 1941 as HMS *Matchless* but, when almost ready for launch, a German bombing raid had blown her from the stocks and destroyed her engine room. Renamed *Mahratta* but carrying the same pennant number (G23) she had to be completely rebuilt. It was bad luck.

Part Two

Across the Room

Further south good luck seemed to continuously attend Eric Goodwin. After her refit in the US, the *Newcastle* returned to the fray and by the middle of 1942 was also involved with convoy duties, but in the warmth of the Mediterranean. If Eric's luck was going to end it seemed likely it would do so now in 'Bomb Alley', the waters between the Axis-held territories of Crete and Libya.

Intent on delivering fuel for the Spitfires based in beleaguered Malta, the convoy of Operation Vigorous sailed from Egypt on 12 June 1942 escorted by minesweepers, corvettes, an old battleship, twenty-six destroyers and eight cruisers including the *Newcastle*. Simultaneously another convoy, Operation Harpoon, sailed for Malta from Gibraltar with the hope of splitting the Axis defences. On 15 June intense German air, submarine and surface attacks were sinking or disabling ship after ship as unwelcome news arrived that a powerful Italian naval force was steaming to close from the north. The situation was deteriorating rapidly as the *Newcastle* took a torpedo in the bows fired by the German E-boat *S-56* operating from Libya. Failing to explode it passed straight through the hull below the waterline, missing by only two feet a tank of aviation fuel the cruiser was carrying. On the forward deck just above, Eric did not immediately realise how close he had come to immolation, being more concerned with emptying his Tommy-gun at a young Stuka pilot who banked his plane low over the ship's deck, his sunlit features clearly laughing in mockery of the frantic efforts of the ship's gunners to bring heavier armament to bear.

That evening attempts to fight through to Malta were abandoned and what was left of the convoy struggled back toward Alexandria, still under attack. By the time safety was reached eight of the merchant ships had been sunk, the remaining three were damaged and numerous escorting warships had also been sunk or damaged. The operation had been an awful failure but Eric had survived. With a makeshift bulkhead the *Newcastle* limped away through Suez and, after stops for further emergency repairs in India, Ceylon, the Cape and Brazil, arrived back in the US in October where, at the Brooklyn Naval Yard, New York, her bows were re-built over the next ten weeks. This time Eric was ready for the mixed grill.

Eventually the restored *Newcastle* returned to England en route for the East. Eric disembarked in Plymouth and was ordered to Queensferry on the Firth of Forth to train in the handling of landing craft in preparation for the D-Day assault on Fortress Europe. He was on his way north when he took two days leave to visit home and called in for a drink at The Butcher's Arms, quite unaware that it was his old mate Jack's wedding day. Still less had he anticipated Agnes.

Beyond the depth of her dark eyes there was something about her Irishness that he felt at home with. Something about her matter-of-fact, easygoing nature that accepted whatever was happening and made the best of it. It was an attitude bred on a poor farm on the cliffs of County Mayo and it touched a chord with Eric (in later years he would often say that he should have been born Irish). Like her elder sister before her, Agnes began a correspondence with a Knodishall boy away at sea, but hers was not in Hong Kong or the Arctic but just past Edinburgh and, leave permitting, could come home on the train. When that happened Agnes, Annie and Hilda would work things in St Albans to get time off together for a few days at Mill House.

That was the case during a week early the following spring, although with husband Jack still away, Annie had decided to stay at work. On Thursday 9 March Hilda and Agnes arranged with Eric to meet at Mill House in the evening and walk to the Leiston Picture House to see Bing Crosby and Dorothy Lamour in *If You Please*, a light-hearted collection of Dixieland music. On the way home the three decided to have a drink in The Volunteer where, at the bar, five American airmen were discussing, as they so often did, the unfamiliar qualities of English beers. The Americans stepped back to open a space for the newcomers: six-foot Eric was wearing his uniform and with an attractive girl on each arm, carried a presence. It was the first time the Americans had seen a Royal Marine uniform, or a Royal Marine, and began to quiz Eric on the subject of his service, largely to take the measure of the obstacle standing between themselves and the two girls. Eric responded in the quietly-toned understatement that was always his manner, bought a pint for himself and gin for the ladies and moved to a table, followed by two of the airmen who had asked if they might join them.

One of the Americans was thinking that he wasn't going to let a single Royal Marine stand between him and a possible date and focused his attention on the girls; the other, though not disinterested in the girls, was also keen to hear Eric's story. Eric recalled some of his more memorable experiences in Massachusetts and New York with factual accuracy – it was not within him to diverge from the truth – which in turn prompted his listener, a newspaperman, to recount exaggerated tales of *his* time in New York. Hilda frequently interrupted both men on points of detail, fascinated by the apparent extremes of the US, from the size of the cars and the mixed grills to the ferocity of the blizzards and the height of the Empire State Building. The newspaperman was impressed. As a natural story-teller he appreciated an attentive audience, and here was a girl who wanted to know more; someone hungry for information but with enough awareness and social skill not to spoil a story with interruption, rather to enhance it. She included everyone in her conversation and was quick to laugh. Very soon the American found he was fascinated by

Hilda. He was Ed Rosenthal and she was everything he had ever dreamt of.

Hilda already had a sweetheart, a soldier named Harry from Liverpool she had met at a dance in Leiston. Or at least Harry liked to think he was her sweetheart. They had met two or three times for a visit to the pub or the Picture House over a period of a month or so before Harry left for North Africa. On parting they had exchanged hugs and a kiss. Thoughts of coming back to Hilda may have subsequently sustained Harry through the heat of the desert campaigns but for Hilda, never short of potential suitors, that had been more or less that: she postponed answering the letters that arrived at Mill House with grains of sand trapped in the gum of the envelopes. Now on leaving The Volunteer to walk home to Knodishall with Eric and Agnes, she saw no reason not to agree to Ed's suggestion that they all meet up again the next day.

Ed had the Friday afternoon off from his job of producing news and stories for the PR department of the 357th and agreed to meet the others after lunch at The Parrot and Punchbowl in Aldringham. The other American, Johny Howlind, would be on duty and graciously bowed out of the arrangements having realised that not even a boat-load of US charm was going to disrupt Agnes's attachment to her Marine, and Ed seemed to have captured Hilda's attention. The four all biked to The Parrot and, after a drink, decided to make the most of the fine, warm afternoon by walking to Thorpeness through the birch-woods.

Soon the two couples were walking separately, Eric and Agnes in front with Ed and Hilda dawdling someway behind as Hilda explained with alternating seriousness and hilarity that the knotty clusters of twigs in the branches of the birch were called 'witches' brooms' and that the little birds flitting around them were tits. They crossed the Saxmundham-Aldeburgh railway line at Sheepwash Cottage and followed the edge of the Mere to Thorpeness where a section of the beach had been cleared of invasion defences. Despite it being only early March, Hilda pulled off her shoes, folded up her slacks and pranced about in the chilly water at the sea's edge as if the water were scalding.

They walked back by the Aldringham Church of St Andrew, wandering through the graveyard inspecting the inscriptions on the numerous Ogilvie tombs, including those of Glencairn Stuart and of his eldest son, the young Alexander, lost at the end of World War I. As Ed had not yet seen an English church at close quarters the foursome entered to inspect the interior where, prompted by a suggestion from Agnes, they sat together for a minute in one of the pews to offer a silent prayer for the safety of loved ones.

Back at The Parrot, reputedly connected to the church by a smugglers' tunnel, it was beginning to get dark. This meant that without lights on his bike, Ed had to cycle off hurriedly as he had to be on duty at 6pm. Before taking his leave he arranged to meet Hilda again the next evening to see the new film at The Picture House. Already he was falling in love. In contrast to the quiet self-containment of Agnes and Eric, Hilda's vivacious girlishness and enthusiastic sociability found a mirror in his own gregarious, enquiring nature. Whether he realised it or not, she was just like his mother.

It was a quiet night for news stories in the small, poorly-heated Nissen hut that housed the duty press room at the base. A central, flat-shaded light bulb lit the yellow and green paintwork of the flimsy hardboard wall lining, while a 'made-on-base' oil-drum stove at one end produced just enough heat to send rivulets of condensation running down the panes of the windows behind the blackout curtains. In the late hours Ed filled in time with another letter to his brother Bob back on Long Island. Newly inspired, he wrote with a personal view of the twin preoccupations of the GI, 'booze and broads'. With no pressure on his time he lectured Bob at length on the differences between an American bar and a British pub, enthusiastically in favour of the more sociable British version as opposed to the ill-lit, heavy-drinking US grottoes populated by depressed men and suspect women. Ed knew well enough that, bars *or* pubs, drinking venues constituted a crucial part of the newspaperman's working environment, making his interest a professional one as much as any other. Here in his first few months in England was beginning a preference for the English way of doing things that was to keep him in Britain for most of his career and eventually create a conflict with the pull of his US roots. On the subject of women, invigorated by his meeting with Hilda, he was equally enthusiastic, stating with a sweeping generality that 'British women are truly intellectual and one does not expect them to play up to men as American women do.'

That perception was most likely engendered by the participants in Anglo-American courtship having very different expectations of the process. As in everything else, the American approach was forthright. Introductions were achieved practically at first sight of a girl by way of easy and open conversation on a train, in a cinema queue or wherever the occasion arose and were frequently simultaneous with a request for a date. Once out with the girl, the smartly uniformed GI, often handsome, usually polite and with a ready flow of compliments, would be generous and attentive and hope, in return, to go as far sexually as the girl might allow. His English date might be appalled by such speedy directness and demur angrily or gracefully. Those blessed with less wisdom than Joyce Leek might mistake flattery for the real thing and be overwhelmed. What was soon discovered was that the Yanks were playing the same old game with new rules, and that putting up a respectability sign with a firm 'no' created no barrier to frequent dating and a hectic social life, especially if a girl was good company.

The GIs for their part were surprised to find that the English girls did not view the dating procedure as the 'kill or be killed' contest that the young American male often perceived it to be, being more interested in having a good time than in jousting on a sexual battlefield. The Americans were impressed by what they saw as a softness and femininity in British women combined with a willingness to please men, attributes they perceived less easily in their American girls. They saw too that the British girls were generally hardworking and experienced in making the most of adverse conditions.

Ed was no exception. After his first proper date with Hilda the next evening he could think of nothing else but this fun-loving, blue-eyed beauty who seemed so different from the girls he had known at home. On the Sunday, Agnes and Hilda had to return to St Albans ready for work on Monday morning. On Wednesday 15 March Ed wrote his first letter to Hilda from Leiston Airfield, suggesting they could meet again during the week of leave he was due from the 22nd. He proposed that perhaps he could come to St Albans and they could go on to a show and dinner in London. Hilda had been to London in the employ of the Agates and for day trips with Agnes and Annie, but the prospect of theatre and dinner was something new: none of her previous beaus had either the money or the confidence for such an adventure.

The Americans had both and, lacking any prior knowledge, entered the most august institutions in search of a good dinner, quite un-awed by name or tradition. Often accompanied by working-class girls, their presence in exclusive establishments previously patronised only by the rich and privileged was resented by snobbish customers and staff alike. Certainly for Ed, approaching thirty and a successful San Francisco newspaperman from a wealthy New York family, seeking out whatever was available by way of high life in the wartime West End came as second nature. For Hilda a new door was opening which her hunger for life well-equipped her to enter. But on this occasion it was not to happen.

The next weekend Eric was still on leave and, eager to rejoin their boyfriends, Hilda and Agnes returned to Mill House on the Friday night. Anne, as the responsible married woman, again stayed behind to earn some extra cash from a weekend shift. In the morning Hilda and Agnes collected Eric from the new council houses on School Road and set off past the school, the church and Peggy's Pond to the railway crossing by Joyce Leek's cottage and onto the airfield where they were to meet Ed. They ambled back later in high spirits brought on by the spring weather, youth, the weekend release from work and a swirling under-current of potential romance. As they approached Mill House the two couples were singing noisily together with the fun of it all when George hurried out to meet them with a drawn face and a telegram in his hand, waving them to silence.

The news had reached Mill House first; official announcement of the *Mahratta's* loss was made later that day. In St Albans Anne Thorpe heard nothing until Agnes got through on the telephone. Matter-of-fact though Agnes might have been she was not going to break this news unless she was with her sister and so told Anne to come down to Knodishall for important news. Her tone betrayed nothing and that evening Anne, anticipating a happy announcement from Agnes and Eric, stepped down from the train in Saxmundham in excited mood, cut short as she read the face of her sister approaching along the platform.

The family's grief was complicated by the fact of Jack's miraculous reappearance after having been officially announced as 'Missing on War Service' two years earlier. This time it was 'Missing Presumed Killed' but if he had done it once, why not again? This should have been answered by a later visit to Mill House by a shipmate of Jack's who had been among the seventeen survivors. He was to explain, gently, that such hopes were futile, as survival of more than a few minutes immersion in the Arctic Ocean was impossible. Yet hope would not surrender. Each day, as she tidied the little living room beside the kitchen, Florrie would lift Jack's photograph from the lace-edged cloth on the sideboard and polish its glass with a corner of her 'pinny' before returning it with a loving, lingering look. Anne too kept faith: polishing his medals, re-reading his letters and never remarrying. At Stone House, where Eric had been born when his father worked for the Wearys, Jack's friend, the flat-capped, red-scarfed village scrap-man 'Tinker' Burrows, took charge of his bicycle. As an official 'man-of-metal' he oiled it up and hung it on the wall of a shed ready for his mate's return. Twenty years later it was still there. Tinker never sold it; the legend established by that first unreported escape would not allow it.

Whatever hope that Anne and Florrie cherished, whatever unlikelihood Tinker Burrows prepared for, Ed knew, and Hilda guessed, that it was futile. In the uncertainty of the war years the unexpected did happen and occasionally survivors from the Russian convoys would show up unexpectedly after having been held *incommunicado* for months in Russian camps while awaiting repatriation. But the odds were all against it, as confirmed to Ed in a letter from his older brother, now serving as a gunnery officer on a US Navy destroyer assisting with escort of the Arctic convoys. 'Do not encourage her to hope,' warned Larry 'there is not a cat-in-hell's chance that he survived unless picked up immediately'. Over that first weekend Ed provided support when he could but had the sense to know when to respect the family's privacy. All knew that grief could not be allowed to stop normal duties continuing: there was a war on and men were being lost every day. With no body to bury at the Knodishall Church of St. Lawrence, Anne, Agnes and Hilda returned to work in St Albans on the Monday and Eric went back to Rosyth. Ed cancelled his leave. Anne's last letter to Jack had been posted in St Albans on 27 February, two days after his death. It came back at the end of April marked 'return to sender on Admiralty instructions'.

Hilda now came home every weekend when she could. Annie sometimes came too but with Eric away, Agnes usually stayed behind. The family found comfort in togetherness. Hilda's priority was to support her parents, particularly Florrie, but she was not the type to be dispirited by grief, and Saturday nights were usually spent out with Ed on a pub crawl or at a dance at the base.

Like Sparkling Wine

Was ever music more wonderful, men so handsome; was the summer really that hot, were the jokes funnier, laughter more merry than at any other time during the World's history?

In 1944 Mill House, in common with most of the houses in Knodishall, was not connected to an electricity supply. Winter eve-nings were lit by a hissing oil lamp and the flickering light of the open fire. In any event, by the time household chores were finished and things readied for the morning, there was little enough time to fill in before bed. What there was might be spent reading or simply gazing contemplatively at the fire's embers until somnolence forced exhausted bodies up the stairs. One weekend Annie brought a wireless set for the household which ran on large accumulator batteries exchanged weekly for newly-charged ones brought round by the ironmonger's van. Florrie and George were delighted with it and listened in each evening but, with or without a wireless, the staid monotony of evenings at home was a powerful incentive for the young at heart to get out and socialise.

It had been The Leiston Picture House that transformed public entertainment at the start of World War I but, at the start of World War II, it was the influx of British and Canadian troops that performed this function by livening up the local dances. The main problem was that the dance bands typically hired for the village halls had lost their younger, more vibrant members to the Forces and tended to be trios or quartets of older men with a preference for old tunes and stringed instruments. This obstacle to modernity was resolved spectacularly when the Yanks arrived on the airfield and began holding dances of their own; the social scene was suddenly electrified.

Early on the night of a base dance one or more US military trucks – quickly christened 'passion wagons' – would pull into the Post Office Square in Leiston to collect the girls responding to the block invitations the Americans would have despatched beforehand to local camps, hostels, work-places or any institution constituting a centre of female population, civilian, military or Women's Land Army. The advance publicity was hardly necessary, for news of a dance spread at speed by word of mouth well before the event. In the early months of the American invasion the more cautious elements of local society made determined efforts to establish a system of chaperoning by means of lists and consents, but any self-appointed authority they might have had was quickly overwhelmed on the night by the increasing excitement and the number of extra girls turning up. Nor did the relaxed attitude of the Americans assist the would-be regulators who were soon forced to abandon their attempts at controlling the fun; no one except the obviously under-age was ever turned away.

For girls determined to catch a Yank a major frustration was the shortage of clothes, fashion accessories, cosmetics and everything else deemed necessary to match up to the glamour of the occasion and the smartly turned out airmen. Hours were spent bent over tedious needlework deconstructing old Sunday dresses for reassembly into something more fashionable. Mixtures of cocoa and coffee were used to stain bare legs before carefully inking seams onto the backs of calves and knees to imitate nylons, at least until a GI could be persuaded to provide the real thing. There were those, precluded by age or disposition from joining in, who looked on disapprovingly, muttering the official line that to dress lavishly was unpatriotic, and predicting – not always incorrectly – trouble ahead. This was where, as one commentator on those times has remarked, 'the warm Gulf Stream of American spontaneity met the iceberg of British reserve, and won.'

Not all the airmen were impressed by the efforts of the ladies. Some, particularly those who had already decided that Suffolk, if not all Britain, was a dirty, backward and freezing hell-hole, could be dismissive. One pilot wrote home

> The English look as if they haven't had any new clothes for years [they hadn't]. For the most part their features are coarse and they know little about using cosmetics. I've yet to see a really neat hair-do. Most of them have ruddy or reddish complexions and there are few neatly dressed women. Their legs, usually bare or in cotton, are often dirty and very muscular, from so much walking I suppose; but a shapely leg is uncommon. Their shoes are usually low-heeled but not well-kept.

This particular testimony could be considered unreliable as he was writing to his wife.

In romance as in war, integrity often suffered in favour of expediency. On 27 April Ed wrote to Hilda in St Albans admitting to having downed several beers with his buddies in the base canteen the previous evening in preparation for an enlisted men's dance, a socially downmarket affair relative to officers' and NCOs' entertainments. The beer, he wrote in a clumsy and snobbish effort to disguise the obvious fun he had enjoyed at the dance, produced the right mood to allow him to 'tolerate' the type of local girl who attended these parties. He goes on to claim that one of these tried to shoulder Hilda aside by confiding that she was already married, and that if Ed didn't believe her then her sister, who knew Hilda well, would produce irrefutable evidence. It was a common ploy, and not without foundation in many cases, but in this one Ed knew better.

On arrival at a major dance on the airfield the girls might each be handed a whole carton of cigarettes, a large box of candy and an elegant corsage. These all came from the base PX stores which dealt in 'shipping' quantities, selling goods in wholesale packaging at subsidised prices. To the GIs it was no big deal; to the British girls it was fabulous. Trained for big dance nights by their high school tradition of proms, the Americans transformed the interior of utilitarian military buildings and hangars into colourful dance halls. Mess tables were disguised under tablecloths laid with flowers and candles, ceilings were hidden with sweeps and swags of brightly-coloured parachute silk, and the lighting was dimmed to a discrete glow. For a country girl it could take the breath away. If the décor didn't then the refreshments would. Side tables were heavy with foods in such variety and abundance as the girls could not have imagined: ham, beef and turkey, tinned peaches and pineapple, huge iced cakes, chocolate, Coca-Cola, marshmallows and ice cream; all seemed to mock the tatty, dog-eared English ration books lying in kitchen drawers at home with no coupons allocated for spare ribs or glazed donuts. 'Gals with pineapple rings on their fingers, juice dripping from their elbows' is one airman's memory.

To this heady mix of handsome men, romantic décor and luxury food was added a final ingredient which would so overwhelm the senses and elevate the soul that all else could for the moment be forgotten – the music. Music that now possesses an unfailing ability to trigger nostalgia for an era when the joy of transient youth flared bright as a match in the hard, dark days of war. For the English girls those nights were magic and for those still alive they remain the most treasured memories of the war, sometimes of their lives.

In 1944 Joan Hunting was eighteen and working in the village post office at Wangford, just to the east of the bomber base at Holton, ten miles north of Leiston. She met her American at a village dance. Jim was a year older and the co-pilot of 'Pin-Up Girl', a Liberator bomber with the 489th Group that had arrived at Holton in April. Joan was writing to two village boys, both serving overseas with the Forces, but Jim was *there*, and more than that, there was an instant understanding – that calm peacefulness in another's company that is not easily found. It expressed itself in laughter but also in silence during day-long cycle rides through the summer countryside. By September Jim had completed his twenty-five missions and returned home to Maine. After the war Joan married one of her correspondents and, in Maine in the same year, Jim also married. They had stolen one short youthful summer together but, knowing they came from different worlds, they each stayed in their own. Both raised families but kept in touch, regularly and openly through the years until Jim died at Christmas 2000 soon after writing 'I wish we had had longer. Do you remember "Long Ago and Far Away"?' It was a song written by Gershwin and Kern, recorded by Glenn Miller and had been playing the night they met: 'just one look and I knew … that all I longed for long ago … was you.'

The official US policy of touring big-name entertainers through theatres of war brought Glen Miller to Parham Airfield seven miles south of Leiston for the 100th Mission celebrations of the 390th Bomb Group on 23 August 1944. 6,000 people turned up, the biggest public gathering in the area since the Hunger March had arrived in Leiston ten years before. The big, brassy sound of his fifty-strong orchestra echoing around a hangar defined the period with numbers such as 'In the Mood', 'Little Brown Jug', 'Moonlight Serenade' and 'Tuxedo Junction'. These were tunes by now familiar to most of the audience for nearly all the US bases had bands of their own – at Leiston it was 'The Buzz Boys' – playing Miller-style swing music heavy with saxophone, music that made it impossible to move rigidly around the dance floor in the old-fashioned way, instead dictated the new style of jitterbug, the forerunner of rock and roll jive. The girls were twirled and whirled over shoulders, through legs and under arms in the now familiar moves of the exuberant dance that, at the time, shook both dance floors and the more conservative onlookers who again attempted to control the fun by placing 'No Jitterbugging' notices around British dance venues, but with little effect. Later in the evening slower numbers by Artie Shaw or Tommy Dorsey would take over, encouraging cheek-to-cheek 'dancing on a dime'.

> he squeezed my hand ... With such an understanding smile and we danced quietly very close ... with a kind of perfect understanding and drowsy companionship through the quiet beat of that song. That remains to this day one of those moments of my life that could have gone on for ever and ever.

That was not said by Joan Hunting but it might have been, or by any one of thousands of young women who experienced the first exciting thrill of romance held tightly in the arms of a Yank.

Oversexed

The sinking of the *Mahratta* had precluded Ed's plans to wine and dine Hilda in London and the gathering pace of military affairs prior to D-Day made further opportunity elusive. Instead, from early April, he was filling daily letters to Waverley Road with romantic expressions of admiration interspersed with occasional reports of life on the Leiston base, as with the story of the attempted assassination of their relationship at the enlisted men's dance. But from 24 May there is a two-week gap in correspondence which had nothing so much to do with the imminence of D-Day as with a dip in that relationship caused by the absence of the easy understanding which Joan Hunting had been so lucky to discover. Certainly the Yanks were fun, a breath of fresh air in grey, run-down England, and that suited Hilda down to the ground. But Ed was almost thirty, Hilda just twenty-three and she was not sure it was time to leave all that she knew behind her. For already, after only two months, that was the direction in prospect: Ed wanted to be serious. And there was the question of sex.

The GIs were not oversexed, it was just that they were unfettered by the inhibitions inherent in British reserve. Unaware of the class divisions so important to the English, and ignorant of the nuances of accent and dress that indicated them, young Americans away at war pursued women indiscriminately. The senior hierarchy of the boys' public school Charterhouse, having invited a group of twelve American officers to stay at the school, was horrified to learn that their guests had, to a man, arranged dates within forty-eight hours of their arrival – all with members of the domestic staff. Later, escorting these ladies to the best venues in London and county, the Americans would be deaf to their working class accents, as they were to the grumbling disapprovals muttered by the self-proclaimed 'superior' classes seated around them.

In 1944 the American writer Mary Lee Settle was attached to the US Office of War Information in London. She writes of two American officers who, having collected a pair of 'Piccadilly Commandos' from the darkness of the street, saw only a dim sign reading 'Bar' and so inadvertently pushed through the labyrinth of heavy blackout curtains into the Tivoli Bar of the Ritz. In the sudden light of that exclusive, elegant room the haggard and dishevelled nature of the ladies was immediately revealed; yet the officers faltered only momentarily as they courteously seated them at a table. Settle reports that the waiter attended 'with all the arrogant politeness' he would have accorded a duchess.

Inevitably the presence of war modified attitudes to courtship. Time might be short, events were unpredictable, and being subject to absolute control from above encouraged servicemen to make the most of opportunities. A man, or woman, could be gone tomorrow, ordered away without warning or, in the case of combat aircrews, be missing in the air over Europe, blown to pieces by flak and cannon shells or, having successfully parachuted from a doomed aircraft, been beaten to death on the ground by enraged German civilians.

The air war was a new and strange sort of warfare. If, during the night, the weathermen confirmed a prospect of reasonable visibility over the target area the air crews would leave their Nissen huts in the cold of the pre-dawn to clamber into jeeps and trucks for the ride out to the dispersed hard-standings where their aircraft loomed, spiky with gun-barrels, from the darkness of the blacked-out base. Ground crews would be finishing tasks of fuelling and arming as the flyers climbed aboard. Then the rural landscape would shudder under a thunderous crescendo as each of the huge planes ignited its four 1,200-horsepower engines and lined up to roar down the runway under full power, struggling to lift full bomb and fuel loads into the air. The sky would fill with lumbering aircraft slowly circling to gain height before assembling formations and heading eastwards over the North Sea to rendezvous with the fighter escorts that would protect them as they droned towards Germany and occupied Europe.

Survivors would come back in the afternoon, crossing low over the coast after a few hours of carnage and high adrenalin, sometimes full of holes with sections of wing or tail or fuselage blown away, often with one or more engines dead or smoking. A red flare fired from the cockpit on approach would signal to the airfield ambulance crews that there were wounded on board. Such aircraft landed last so as not to risk blocking the runway with wreckage. Ground crew and friends would watch from the area of the control tower, sucking in their breath and holding it behind gritted teeth as a twenty-something pilot nursed down a damaged plane, dipping and lurching onto the runway, its young crew wet with blood and the sweat of fear. Hope for the ten men of a missing crew waned with passing hours. If their plane's loss had not been observed there was a chance of recovery from an emergency landing at another airfield, or even from a ditching at sea but, if by nightfall there was no news, grim assumptions were usually correct.

After debriefing and a meal in the mess a returned crew might be back down at the local that evening enjoying a drink with the regulars as if nothing much had happened. Men found release from the tension in different ways. At Wangford, Olly – the navigator on Jim's bomber crew – would call at Joan Hunting's house in the evening after a mission to shut himself in the front room with the family's piano. He would play for hours. Others would roll home drunk, or seek out loose women, or write long letters to loved ones.

Each base ran itself as a small town busily preoccupied with the business of sustaining a community of 2,000–3,000 men. The war zone was well out of sight and for many personnel could be out of mind, combat missions seeming to happen a long way away in strange isolation from the normal life of the base for which they were the *raison d'etre*. Yet for flying crews the constant roar of engines being tested or the sudden penetrating announcement from the airfield tannoy during the afternoon before a mission – 'Attention! Attention! The following officers and crews report to the briefing room immediately' – kept them all too conscious of the danger. As were those ground crew patching holes or scrubbing away at pools of dried blood. Some bomb groups lost almost 2,000 men during their brief stay in East Anglia. Leiston lost eighty-two of its fighter pilots during a twenty-month occupation by the Americans. In such circumstances it was understandable that in their determination to seize the day the airmen sometimes felt there was insufficient time to observe all the formalities of courtship.

A few of them were happy to employ the services of the professional women that infiltrated the bases after taking the train up from London and Ipswich. Others employed no more than a very direct approach, such as they would never dare attempt at home, confident in the general GI assumption that English girls were 'easy'. In some cases it was more a case of a girl being simply unnerved by the ability of a forthright American to talk unabashedly about sex, and ask for it. Harry Crosby, a pilot with 'The Bloody 100th' Bomb Group (so called because it lost 200 aircraft and eighty-six per cent of its original crews) attended an Anglo-American liaison conference where one female American WAC officer theorised that whereas US dating rituals trained girls to say 'no', British boys did not usually choose to push their luck early on in the dating game with the result that British girls had no experience of rejecting forthright advances, and thus often conceded without resistance.

For many, resistance was the last thing on their minds, for the Yanks were an awful temptation. After long shifts of monotonous war work in a drab society dulled by years of shortages and relentless econo-mies, the lure of a little glamour could be irresistible. Hurtling around the dance floor doing the jitterbug or swaying in the arms of a tall and handsome American was as close to heaven as a girl could hope to get. The GIs earned more in a week than the locals did in a month; they hailed taxis and frequented the best hotels; they had impossible-to-get food and luxuries and they approached life with exuberance and good humour. As a Home Office report of 1945 put it:

> To girls brought up on the cinema, who copied the dress, hair styles and manners of Hollywood stars, the sudden influx of Americans, speaking like the films, who actually lived in the magic country, and who had plenty of money, at once went to the girls' heads. The American attitude to women, their proneness to spoil a girl, to build up, exaggerate, to talk big, and to act with generosity and flamboyance, helped to make them the most attractive boyfriends.

If some women perceived that the price of a GI-sponsored holiday from drudgery was promiscuity then there were those happy to pay, though in many cases promiscuity would be too strong a word for the female sexual liberation that was beginning as an unintended by-product of the war. Developing in parallel with female emancipation from unremitting domesticity, it was encouraged by the removal of women from the home to the factory, field and auxiliary forces, and reflected a desire to make the most of fleeting wartime opportunities. For soldiers military adventures abroad had always been accompanied by sexual ones when opportunity arose, but what was sauce for the gander was becoming sauce for the goose.

For the most part the Americans were 'easy', ready to generate a whirl of gaiety and generosity, neither asking nor giving long-term commitment, nor indulging in tiresome farewells when the time came. Most significantly, as Joan Hunting had realised, they were here while most British men, husbands or boyfriends, were away on active duty. Harry Crosby remarked 'Maybe never in history was there so perfect a fit between the women that men needed and the men that women needed'.

The fit might have been perfect but colour was a problem when the women were white and the men black. Of more than a million GIs temporarily resident in Britain, some 130,000 were African Americans with 12,000 of these in the Eighth Air Force. Not that they were permitted to actually fly aircraft, or even work on them as ground crew. Segregation and racism was endemic in the US and General 'Hap' Arnold, in command of the country's air forces, was no liberal prepared to relax these policies in a time of war: such a move would have resulted in civil war amongst his troops. Segregation continued in England as it did at home, with black Americans quartered in separate accommodation areas on the bases, their duties restricted to construction, transport and logistics. Socially segregation was maintained by a system of 'black and white' nights, whereby off-base passes were released to blacks one night, whites the next. Certain pubs were designated 'black' and others 'white', the former often less salubrious, or less convenient to the base.

This all created a problem for those responsible for the formulation of British policy towards the new allies. Segregation was illegal in Britain, or perhaps more accurately non-existent, given a virtually homogenous population containing only some 8,000 blacks, and Home Secretary Herbert Morrison was anxious that British police should play no part in its application. Churchill, on the other hand, was anxious to avoid creating any difficulties with the Americans. The official line thus became that while on base US rules would apply, off-base British law would take precedence. The reality was that, in rural areas at least, British police did support American policy in matters such as the segregation of pubs on the purely pragmatic grounds that, had they not, they would have been unable to cope with the resulting chaos as black and white set about each other.

Trouble really started when English girls, innocent of any racial prejudice and sometimes just curious, began dating black GIs. From the girls' point of view one GI was, *prima facie*, as good as the next, irrespective of colour. For the black GIs their open acceptance by the ladies, and by British society generally, was a refreshingly new situation. But nothing was guaranteed to inflame white segregationalist Americans more than the sight of a black soldier escorting a white woman. A detachment of black Americans was based with the 390th Bomb Group at Parham and Herbert Meadows, employed on the adjacent farm, recalls a vicious fight erupting in the village street when one of these men was ambushed by a group of whites intent on 'teaching him a lesson' after he was seen out walking with a local girl. Such overt racism did not go down well with the English whose sense of fair play was offended to the extent that some, including the girls, made a point of being particularly hospitable to the black soldiers.

Despite the lack of prejudice from the English the prospect of a mixed marriage between a black GI and an English girl was virtually nil, as such a relationship was illegal in many US states and almost unknown in a Britain yet to become multicultural. In the awkward situation of a mixed-race pregnancy the absence of legally-endorsed segregation on this side of the Atlantic was no real protection – convention and the homogenous nature of the population attaching such debilitating stigma to both the resulting child and its mother that almost invariably the infant was taken into institutionalised care and the father returned to the US post-haste.

A particular problem adding to the generally racy image of the Americans was that nowhere was there much in the way of domestic privacy. Sex *al fresco* was often the only solution and 'Marble Arch' style against a wall or in a doorway – as offered by the 'Piccadilly Commandos' – frequently exposed the Yanks to further disapproval.

In the countryside around the airfields privacy was a little easier to find, at least in summer, though not everyone troubled to find it. At Leiston, George Watson, a teenager cycling home to his parents' farm after an evening at the pictures, ended up in a bramble-thick ditch after executing a violent evasive manoeuvre to avoid running over a GI and his girl horizontal in the road. It was at least dark.

Pause for Thought

The truth was that whatever generalities might have been justified, the responses of partners to new relationships were as much a matter of individual choice in war as in peacetime, remaining personal and varied. Hilda had heard all the stories and warnings and knew friends with bitter tales to tell. That didn't worry her; she was confident of Ed's sincerity. Agnes and Eric and Florrie were too. That was really the problem. Not that she was a dilettante, shy of commitment, but more the reverse, in that her strong personal ethics would allow her only so far without it, and was a thirty-year-old transient American soldier really what she wanted? As Joan Hunting and Jim understood, a marriage would not be of just two people, but of two worlds. On the evening of the last Saturday in May, standing in the dark by the little iron gate that led to the front door of Mill House, she told Ed of her doubts and gently rebuked his over-exuberant courtship. The next day she wrote to apologise for any hurt that conversation had caused. Two days later she wrote again to reiterate her position but also mentioned that the red roses he had sent the previous week were not quite dead.

It was not a breakdown, more a pause for consideration before things went too far. On 4 June, two days before D-Day, Ed responded to Hilda's two letters of the previous week with a letter admitting that yes, perhaps he had been an insensitive fool in pushing for too much too soon. Ruefully he accepts a 'just friends' situation. Two weeks later, on the eve of his thirtieth birthday, he writes again, wistfully acknowledging the new arrangement and goes on to fill the

letter with news rather than the sweet nothings of before. As a professional correspondent this came easily but, pointedly, on this occasion
the 'news' suggests that not all the sexual predators are American.

Ed relates that, while in London on leave during the week following D-Day and hungry for insights from France, he was drinking
with some GIs in the bar of the Regent Palace Hotel when the group
was accosted by a girl intent on celebration. She claimed to have
come straight from the law courts on the Strand after being acquitted
of poisoning her wealthy husband: her defence counsel had somehow
persuaded the jury the man had poisoned himself. In this counsel had
been aided by the deceased's obsessively jealous behaviour in record-
ing in his diary every trivial detail of his wife's activities, minute by
minute, from the time of her waking to the moment of her falling
asleep. The suggestion was that his inability to maintain such an obviously impossible task, albeit self-appointed, engendered such depths
of suspicion as he was unable to bear.

It seemed as if his worries might have been well-founded, for after
warning Ed to beware the 'B.T.O.' (Big-Time-Operator) girls who
hunted the better London hotels, the acquitted introduced him to a
female 'friend' who claimed to have been married twice to officers,
both of whom were now missing in action with insurance paid up.
Telling Ed that he was the most interesting man she had ever met, the
first girl then departed, leaving him with her phone number and her
friend. Ed said that he left the first on the bar; mindful of poison, he
probably did. Whether he left the friend there as well following her
unlikely claims he fails to record, but adds that the poisoner's story
was confirmed by the next day's papers, some way behind reports of
Hitler's new secret weapon – the V1 flying bombs that had just begun
to inflict a new wave of death and destruction on Londoners.

Ed's next fortnightly letter was written on 1 July still in 'friends'
mode and puts a brave but consciously wistful spin on a description
of the night of his thirtieth birthday, Sunday 18 June, which had been
spent on a lonely guard duty on Leiston airfield, walking his post and
musing on his increasing age under a starlit sky. He hadn't known it
but on that Sunday morning a V1 had demolished the Guards Chapel

in Kensington with such horrendous loss of life that the news had been withheld.

His next letter was written mid-afternoon on Monday 24 July and is altogether different, not because of tragic news but because Hilda had telephoned him at noon that day. 'Remember me?' she had begun in a quiet voice in which Ed detected both humility and defiance. She told him that she had been at Mill House since the previous Saturday. At first he felt wounded by the realisation that she had been in Knodishall over the weekend without making contact. But then they had agreed to meet that night at The Parrot and during the afternoon Ed typed a single side of flimsy press-office paper to hand to her that evening. It was a statement of his feelings, a sort of insurance — as he explained in it — against the possibility that, amid the emotional swirl of their first meeting for two months, he would fail to communicate his deepest thoughts as accurately as he could by writing them down in the calm of the office. He professes his love, says how much he has missed her, praises her sense and apologises for his foolishness. He wants to be with her, this time on her terms, content to allow events to take their course slowly and naturally into the future.

It worked, and the two spent most of the rest of that week together. On the following Sunday night, just after Hilda had returned to St Albans, Ed was in happy mood and allowed Wesley, his colleague in the press room, to type his next letter to her on the comic pretence that, as Wesley had never had a girlfriend, he had never written a love-letter and needed to know how it was done. Wesley inserts parenthesised comments of his own into the dictated letter bemoaning its brevity, the absence of mushy love-talk and advising that, if he were the recipient, he would certainly have nothing to do with the sender.

Hilda might have smiled at the tomfoolery but ignored the advice and now in the last week of July, after the false start of the spring, she began a courtship with Ed that with an accelerating turmoil of parties, new friends and good times would open the doors on a new world.

Gold Beach

At 130 Waverley Road the three young women lodging with land-lady Mrs Izzard were now all deeply committed to their men in one way or another. Hilda's sister-in-law Anne – now nearly twenty-eight – could not accept that she had been widowed after less than three months of marriage. There was no body, no confirmation of the death and, until that happened, she would continue to believe that Jack was not dead, that he would somehow miraculously re-appear from the frozen Arctic as he had from the jungles of Burma. But deep inside her an icy void was growing with the knowledge that this was not so much a belief as a hope, a hope that died a little more with each passing day. Anger took root in that void to challenge the youthful playfulness that had once ruled Anne, and it grew to a sharp, resigned bitterness that the war had cheated her of a great love.

Her sister Agnes was luckier and happier and, like Hilda, four years younger. Agnes was now in love with the man she had met in Knodishall on the evening of Anne's wedding day, the handsome, gentle Royal Marine, Eric Goodwin. With the approach of D-Day Eric had left the training base on the Firth of Forth to transit the Forth-Clyde canal as one of the four-man crew of a 'Landing Craft Assault' en route to embark on the 'Landing Ship Infantry' S.S. *Empire Mace* which was waiting at Greenock. With the LCAs and their crews taken aboard, the *Empire Mace* sailed for the south coast, training continuing at various locations on the way. At Weymouth Eric's LCA acted as post-boat, distributing mail to the growing flotillas of ships waiting in the harbour to load the mass of troops and armour assembling in the hinterland. Finally in the Solent, the *Empire Mace* received her full complement of men and craft and, with all 'sealed' aboard, her task was revealed – to land the Green Howards on Gold Beach. After a weather delay of twenty-four hours she weighed anchor at 5.45pm on 5 June to join the armada bound for France, and by first light was hove to seven miles off the Normandy coast.

In the grey chill the Geordie soldiers of the Green Howards clambered down scramble nets into the flat-bottomed LCAs that had been lowered from the ship and now lay alongside, rolling wildly in the heavy swell. Each took thirty or so men. Those who had not already succumbed aboard the *Mace* were soon overwhelmed by seasickness. As the history of D-Day has recorded, the sea that morning was horribly rough, sinking amphibious tanks with whole crews and drowning soldiers weighed down by full kit. Eric took his first 'lift' in just after 7am, a platoon of Green Howards under the command of a major carrying a small rucksack from which protruded the neck of a full bottle of Hennessey cognac. Suddenly, feeling brandy might be superfluous in the circumstances, the major presented the bottle to Eric just before reaching the beach, saying it would only get broken. In the event it was high tide and the LCA went in over the top of the beach defences without mishap.

By the time Eric came in with a second 'lift' at 11am, approaching low water brought the LCA up against the projecting barriers, each pole tipped with a mine. Despite the difficult sea conditions the crew got the vessel in through a gap cleared by the engineers. Subsequent trips beached supplies for what was a relatively straightforward landing compared to the carnage occurring in other sectors and the Howards penetrated well inland through the course of the day. But 'relatively' does not mean without bodies floating in the water. With the aid of a boathook Eric and his crew hauled one unconscious young soldier into the LCA. He appeared unhurt and they struggled to pump the water from his chest until one of them noticed a pearl of blood appear from a small bullet hole just behind his ear. Sewn into a canvas hammock he was later committed to the sea from the *Mace*. When twilight finally closed that long day, Eric's LCA lay alongside the landing ship as he hosed the last of the morning's vomit out through the scuppers into the darkening Channel. Within the week he was back in the Solent writing to Agnes.

The Romance Strengthens

The first days of August were grey and cold but the weather could not dent Ed's romantic euphoria. On the 3rd he wrote to Hilda again to report the events of a night out with his friend 'Tanner' to celebrate the latter's promotion to First Lieutenant. After cycling to Aldringham to drop off their washing with a 'laundry lady', they had primed themselves at The Parrot before continuing to a dance in Leiston where they found Nancy Moore and Molly Felgate. Previously introduced to Nancy via the Hilda connection, 'Tanner' had begun a relationship which had gone awry, and now pointedly danced with Nancy's mother while ignoring her daughter. Molly was with another friend of Ed's, a GI called Gordon, that she too had met through Hilda, but by the end of the evening these two had also fallen out, leaving Hilda the only one of the old Knodishall gang going steady with a Yank.

By the time Hilda returned from St Albans for the weekend the weather had changed. She spent most of Saturday swimming and sun-bathing with Ed at Thorpeness before they biked to The Parrot and then on to the base dance where Ed's friends all affected to swoon at her feet, his romantic credibility having soared with the landing of this local Venus. On the way back to Mill House the warmth and stillness of the summer night suggested to Hilda a return to the beach at Thorpeness, where they skinny-dipped in the moonlight. Sunday was spent at Mill House where Annie, with sub-versive winks at Hilda, teased Ed remorselessly in front of George and Florrie as to the whereabouts of his damp swimming costume until, quite out of character, George interjected 'Don't be so silly Anne – I shouldn't think they worried about costumes at that time of night!' whereupon Florrie began to colour and busied herself with the lunch.

After they had eaten Hilda suggested to Ed he pay his respects to Charlie and Alice, distant at their end of the house down that long unlit corridor. Ed had of course met the grandparents in the spring, and had shared his sympathies after the *Mahratta* was lost, but now he could renew the acquaintance. Hilda went first to make sure all was well and that they would be welcome. A moment later she reappeared, beckoning from the square of light at the end of the corridor. Ed emerged to find the grandparents and Clifford seated in three rockers spaced around the small, dark kitchen, set back from the oil-clothed table where lay the remains of dumplings and beef. All three were waking from a post-dinner snooze. Only Charlie rose to his feet to greet the visitor warmly. There was no talk of the war, only the weather and the poor size of the potatoes that year. Hilda spoke with Alice about George's work constructing shuttering in the training areas. Clifford butted in with unfocused questions about the US until Alice told him not to be so silly, whereupon he shut up entirely, and Hilda went out to fetch a pail of water from the rain-water tank for the washing up. Stooping back under the low doorway to the corridor Ed left that gloomy room stirred and excited, not just by the fact of his romance with Hilda but by an awareness of the contrasts with his Long Island upbringing and by this whole English adventure. He always had an eye for the bigger picture.

Brimming with life after that weekend, Ed felt compelled to write to his younger brother in New York with news of his happiness. Describing the cycling, sun-bathing and swimming by day and night he reports that the North Sea after dark is pretty cold but, as Hilda had dashed straight in, the situation had left him with no option but to follow (there are rectangular holes in the letter where the censor has cut out the words *North Sea* and *Thorpeness*). He is lyrical about her inner and outer beauty, although he betrays an absence of botanical knowledge, and manages to perplex his brother and family, by strangely describing her hair as 'like heather'.

Difference in eating habits was a frequent source of mutual amusement to both GIs and the English and, writing of George and Florrie, Ed praises their generosity and adds:

> They live in a little house across from the village green. Every time I walk in they are either just finishing or just sitting down to tea and insist I have some with them. 'Tea' really means supper. If you drink your tea but don't eat the sandwiches and cakes, the hostess says 'Have some more tea' meaning, eat some more. It's confusing alright.

Love, Sex and Lies

The pattern was set for the rest of that summer with Hilda returning to Knodishall at weekends for fun and games with Ed and a lively group composed of his GI buddies intent on having a good time and her childhood friends determined to overcome any temporary setbacks in catching a Yank of their own. Occasionally Agnes and Anne came up with her from St Albans but with Agnes loyal to Eric – now busy on the South Coast with Operation Pluto movements – and Anne futiley waiting for Jack, the Irish girls were largely out of the party.

Such fidelity was not necessarily the norm. A British Army medical officer presented statistics to a wartime committee showing that a wife's faithfulness would survive an average of two years of her husband's absence before lapsing. Notably he offered no view on the length of a husband's loyalty, that not being seen as such a potential social problem. Nor was it only British husbands and boyfriends who suffered competition at home while away on duty: many GIs received 'Dear John' letters from wives and girlfriends in the States. One airman based in Norfolk recalled

> the letters started arriving from wives who had got tired of waiting. Of thirty-six men in my barracks, fourteen received 'Dear Johns'. I was lucky in a way. I had no children but the older men had the pictures of their children by their bunks and lived for the daily mail-call.

Ed's weekday letters to Waverley Road kept Hilda up to date with social developments in the aftermath of the previous Saturday nights and gave the latest from the mid-week Aero Club dances. Nancy Moore received a good deal of reportage. In fact Nancy had married inadvisedly at the start of the war and, with her husband absent in Italy, was anxious to recover some ground while she could. As proprietor of Knodishall's only garage and taxi service, with access to rationed fuel supplies, she was well placed for GI interaction. 'Tanner', John, 'Muscles' and 'Fuzzy' all make the news in Ed's coverage of the vagaries of Nancy's love life, though none seemed to measure up as after the war she was re-married to an Englishman from the Royal Engineers.

Reaction to wartime infidelities, as with attitudes to sex, were varied and individual, but Americans were often surprised by the tolerance of British husbands who might observe the flirtatious dalliance of a wife with equanimity, whereas the energy of male American culture would demand an aggressive show of proprietorial rights. Joyce Leek's husband Bill did not dance – he was a champion darts player instead – but he voiced no objection to Joyce dancing the night away with Jeff at the airfield parties. Jeff admitted to having a wife back home and, though he fancied Joyce, he behaved with honour. The fact that Joyce and Bill were in love and, more to the point, that Bill was at home in a reserved occupation, must have helped him.

Other married women were far too mindful of their reputations, and fearful of village gossip, to dally with the Americans. In a letter dated 9 August Ed reported to Hilda that, having found Eric's sister Winnie at a dance in Leiston, he had started to walk her home but on reaching the public road Winnie had dismissed him, saying it would not do for a married woman to be seen with an American, and certainly not by the eyes of her diminutive husband Jimmy Atkins. She was probably right because Nancy Moore remembers seeing Jimmy squaring up to an enormous American one night outside the Knodishall Hut, having accused him of flirting with Winnie at the dance being held inside. Fortunately for the tiny Jimmy, onlookers concerned for his survival intervened to calm the situation.

The risk of village censure did not inhibit another married acquaintance of Ed's, a blonde, petite Knodishall girl called Chrissie Lord who lived with her mother in Hunt's Barn Cottages on the Leiston Road. Raised through the Depression years with no father and very little household income, Chrissie had had a tough early life from which she sought escape when the coming of war presented the opportunity to marry a Yorkshire soldier stationed on the coastal defences. Ed had met both of them while drinking with his buddies in The Volunteer. He had become engrossed in conversation with the Yorkshireman about life in the US. But Chrissie had been more interested in making eyes at the other GIs at the bar, for the arrival of the Yanks had made it clear to her that she had made her move too soon and so missed the better deal. Now she desperately sought to recover the situation, the presence of a husband providing no deterrent to beginning an adulterous relationship with at least one American. But amid the feast of opportunities brought about by the combination of her good looks and the presence of the USAAF, she was unable to keep her head. In a letter to Hilda dated 11 August Ed reports that at the previous night's dance at the airfield's Red Cross Club a vicious fight had erupted between the drunken Chrissie and her equally intoxicated American M.P. boyfriend. This had turned really nasty when the boyfriend pulled a knife on his fellow, but sober, M.P.s who were trying to pull him off the battered Chrissie. Ed doubts she will ever be allowed on the base again as 'every time she visits there is some kind of brawl.' Not long after this incident the husband attempted to kill himself, was invalided out of the army and returned to Yorkshire. Hilda Spoore, who was a close neighbour in Knodishall, remembers him as a 'very nice man'.

As a newspaperman Ed was no stranger to alcohol himself and on 28 September he reported to Hilda on another Aero Club dance at which his love for whisky might have led to an amorous liason of the more usual kind. With the dance employing a visiting band inferior to the 'Buzz Boys' and, unusually, suffering from an inadequate number of attractive girls, Ed was focused on imbibing his share of a bottle of White Horse scotch which his buddy Griff had managed to purchase the previous week. Decent whisky was in short supply and Griff had the bottle concealed, boot-leg style, in a brown paper bag when he spotted two likely ATS girls by the door. Although they were well-attended by GIs, Griff managed to lure one away with a promise of free whisky. Joined by another buddy called Robinson, the group of four ducked into the darkened base theatre where Griff announced to the girl that every drink would cost her a kiss. She had quite a few drinks and they enjoyed quite a few kisses, but when Griff became so drunk he started kissing Ed in the dark by mistake, Ed stumbled out of the cinema, shortly followed by the ATS girl who said 'Those boys are far too drunk' and suggested the two of them go for a walk. Ed claims that with Hilda always in his mind he walked her only as far as the canvas-topped army truck ferrying the girls back to Leiston, but adds that she kissed him goodnight as if she hadn't seen a man in ten years. The ATS girl was simply out for an evening's fun, but some English girls expected a lot more and could be badly deceived.

Only hours after war had been declared on 3 September 1939 a lone inbound aircraft crossing the Essex coast over Westcliffe-on-Sea triggered the first air-raid alert of the conflict. Despite having flown from Germany it was in fact friendly, but nonetheless the authorities decided the level of risk was such that all those residents with young children should be immediately evacuated. With her infant son twenty-year-old Eileen English was sent to London the next morning. Within a year the Blitz had made the capital a good deal more dangerous than the coast and Eileen decided that the child's safety would be best served if he was looked after by her mother-in-law in Yoxford.

Eileen visited from London whenever she could through the war and so observed the romance that developed between her sister-in-law 'Girlie' and Tom, a handsome Captain of the 357th on Leiston airfield. Superficially the relationship seemed similar to Ed and Hilda's. Tom, too, was from New York, was sophisticated, educated and wealthy, a matching partner to the beautiful, vivacious Girlie. The two were inseparable and appeared deeply in love. The difference was that Tom was already married, a truth which, unbetrayed by his fellows, he managed to conceal from Girlie until the day of his homeward departure from Leiston. Girlie, who was preparing herself for marriage and emigration to the US as a GI bride, was devastated. On the rebound she married the dependable, patient, but unexciting Percy Leicester, an English artilleryman she had known from before the war. It was not a love match.

A 'sugar-daddy' relationship and a second marriage followed in later years. The first loves were unforgettable, but not always simply because of the romance.

On a warm June night in 1944, during a dance at the airfield Red Cross Club, an inebriated nineteen-year-old shop assistant called 'Buttie' Newson stumbled into the darkness outside the building supported by the arms of a GI she had met inside. A few minutes later, pinned against a tree in the woods behind the base parachute store, she conceived a child. Later, when her condition became apparent, Buttie's chapel-going mother was horrified and realising that any attempt to confront the airman was hopeless – Buttie couldn't even remember what he looked like – arranged for her daughter to be sent away to an aunt in Sittingbourne where, for as long as she was able, she helped in the hop-yards with the Women's Land Army. A year later, with the war over and the Americans gone from Leiston, Buttie returned to her parents' terraced cottage with her infant daughter Mary who, to escape the stigma of illegitimacy, was presented to the world as her new baby sister. Nobody was fooled except perhaps the baby, but nothing was said too loudly and the deceit continued.

In 1949 Buttie married a hard-drinking Garrett's labourer named Fred Clarke, moved into his rented 'two-up-two-down' on Kitchener Road and bore him two children, Tom and Janet. By now the lies were too difficult to undo and her first-born Mary, who grew into an overweight and reclusive girl, continued to live with her 'parents' unaware that they were really her grandparents. Years later, during the awful hard winter of 1962/3, her 'father', a railwayman with the L.N.E.R., died after being crushed by a coal wagon in the Ipswich yards. On 16 March of that spring, with the thaw finally underway, Buttie organised a family supper to celebrate Mary's eighteenth birthday. Tom and Janet, now thirteen and twelve, had wrapped small presents for their 'aunt' and were blowing up balloons when Mary and Gran arrived.

The party had to get underway without Fred who had been told earlier that day that, for various reasons of re-organisation, he no longer had a job at Garrett's which, by the 1960s, was in a terminal decline. Consequently he was behind a pint glass in the Engineer's Arms and eventually arrived home in a sorry state. The earfull he then received from Buttie proved the final provocation of his day, releasing a torrent of drunken self-pity including much bellowing about secrets and lies from which Mary belatedly discerned the truth of her parentage.

Amid the shouted accusations and confessions that followed, the shy Mary, inflamed by her real mother's betrayal, disclosed that she had been sexually abused by her supposed 'father'. This information came as no shock to the guilt-ridden Buttie who had already guessed as much, having received the same treatment herself. In the explosion that resulted on the release of three decades of emotional repression the family was blown apart. Mary realised she had never had a real father; God-fearing Gran was exposed to the truth about her deceased husband; Buttie never forgave herself, nor Fred, from whom she was eventually divorced; and not least hurt were the young Tom and Janet who, having fled upstairs to escape the screaming and shouting, now had to accept that their aunt was their half sister. A few years later they fled further by emigrating to Australia.

For Mary her missing father became her Holy Grail, the figure who might give her the parental love she felt she had been denied. Buttie thought she remembered that his name had been Rod or Rodger but refused to talk about it, as did Tom and Janet in Australia, insisting the past was best left alone. After Buttie died in 2003 Mary became desperate to trace her father, but all research proved fruitless. Now she is resigned to the fact that, sixty-three years after her conception, she will never know him.

It is quite likely that, given the circumstances of the conception, he might well have not wanted to know *her*, at least not in 1945, and, if that was so, he would have escaped many of the pressures to admit paternity that come to bear in peacetime. Not that illegitimacy was acceptable during the war: in the social context of the 1940s it was held as a stigma blacking mother, child and wider family alike and, if possible, was quickly legalised by a timely marriage; hidden by an adoption; removed by an illegal abortion; or disguised by a husband accepting another man's child. It was not spoken of openly. But inevitably a 'live today for tomorrow we die' recklessness, as encouraged by the hardships and uncertainties of war, combined with the presence of glamorous well-paid Yanks increased the problem no end.

The particular difficulty with the honourable solution of marriage was that GI fathers were transients, and if not killed in Europe they were shipped back to the US. Once home they were inclined to put wartime experiences behind them as they began new civilian lives, most of them at this point still in their early or mid-twenties. Official US policy was complicit in such evasive action by discouraging cross-cultural marriages as counter to military interests and unpopular with the US electorate. Consequently an Anglo-American marriage required the consent of the GI's commanding officer which, with official sanction, was often withheld or administratively delayed while the GI, especially if he so requested, was posted elsewhere. Expectant mothers seeking help or information from the US military establishment were often met by an obstructive cavalier attitude that held 'soldiers will be soldiers'. Tearful tales of jilted promises and real hardship were frequently answered with a cold 'Well, that's too bad ma'm, but that's war'.

Returning British husbands might occasionally be unsuspecting that a child was not their own if a period of leave made sense of it, but usually the truth would out sooner or later with unpredictable consequences – divorce; acceptance and forgiveness; or a damaged and unhappy marriage. As always – as was the case with the war itself – it would be the children who inherited difficulties not of their own making: growing up without fathers, or discovering eventually that 'Dad' was not *really* that, and then having to deal with the anger aroused by the deceit and rejection. This legacy of emotional trauma left incubating in the wake of the GIs has persisted indelibly through the decades, making it perhaps the most lasting impact of their brief presence.

Moving On

As Ed's romance with Hilda gathered pace so did his army career. Since arriving in England most of his time had been spent in the draughty Nissen huts and spartan military offices of Leiston airfield. On duty he wrote PR stories for the air force. Off duty he cycled to Leiston to deliver his washing to one of the local ladies providing a laundry service and drank with his buddies at the base PX, the Aero Club or at the local pubs. He had met the local girls, and Hilda; had fun at the dances and been to the pictures. He had become acquainted with fish and chips, the local people and the surprisingly primitive living conditions of rural Suffolk. He had spent freezing nights on guard duty in the mud and frost of his first winter overseas, a winter that coated the bleak expanses of the new airfield with ice and snow, mocking efforts to keep warm beside the small iron stoves which equipped the base hutments. He was a good newspaperman, and that translated well to his PR duties. It was a skill that had not gone unnoticed and now, in the autumn before his second winter in England, word came through to Leiston that he was wanted by the PR office at Eighth Air Force Headquarters, High Wycombe.

Over the first weekend of October Hilda came home to Knodishall as Ed prepared to leave Leiston. On the Saturday night, with the young Americans in their snappy uniforms and the girls in frocks and lipstick, the 'old' gang of the past summer laughed and drank their way from The Parrot to The Volunteer and back to the base. Ed was sorry to be leaving his buddies of his first year in England, but by 1944 people were more than accustomed to sudden rearrangements of social life caused by new postings announced with little or no warning. On the plus side High Wycombe was a lot closer to St Albans.

Ed spent Sunday at Mill House with the family before Tanner showed up in a local taxi on his way to Saxmundham and offered Hilda a lift to the station. He was accompanied by a Land Girl he had met the previous evening who needed to get back to Ipswich.

Ed went with them and, after seeing Hilda off on the train, was dropped back at Mill House, where his presence was noticed by two young evacuee boys of about five and eight. As George lit a fire for the evening and Florrie prepared some 'tea' the boys knocked at the back door to ask if 'the soldier' would be interested in buying the second-hand bicycle pump the smaller of the two was holding. As a bicycle was Ed's personal transport, and a spare pump being useful, he said 'yes' and inquired the price. 'Fifteen shillings' blurted out the youngest boy. This was met by a burst of laughter from George and Florrie behind him who knew, that as a new pump cost about two shillings, the boys were trying to 'con' the Yank. Badly discomfited the salesman claimed his older brother had told him to ask that much. In any event, Ed knew how much beer fifteen shillings would buy, so declined the purchase and, after tea, cycled back to the base for the last time. The following day he moved from the 1076th Signals Company, Leiston F373 to High Wycombe and the focus of his social life moved to London.

London

By the end of 1944 London was a tired and worn-out city, physically and psychologically. Everywhere desolate gaps in rooflines marked where bombs had reduced treasured homes to piles of brick rubble and blackened joists. Like the skins of burst drums, segments of first floors hung at angles from once-private bedroom walls, now exposed to the weather and public view. Feeling vaguely voyeuristic, passers by averted their eyes from rain-drenched wallpaper, once carefully smoothed, now flapping in the wind.

Without maintenance elegant facades peeled, faded and rusted. Dirty walls of stained sandbags blighted public buildings. The smell of damp plaster, brick dust and coal smoke hung in the winter air. At night the blackout, eased to a 'dim-out' in September, had brought a country darkness to the city, but one filled with the human noise of voices, shouts and footsteps, and of vehicles, with their headlights masked to narrow slits, feeling their way along unlit streets.

And with the dirt and dark and neglect there remained a mute, unacknowledged backcloth of fear, ignored but insidiously exhausting. After the passing of the 1940-41 Blitz and the 'mini-Blitz' of early 1944, Londoners had slept more easily, though many still preferred to sleep beneath the streets, sprawled on the grimy platforms of the Tube stations, some for their fourth year. Then the onslaught of the V1s in the summer followed by the V2s of the autumn sent thousands more underground. During the day the tedium of wartime life carried on regardless, for there was little choice and *sangfroid* was obligatory. Mary Lee Settle wrote of lunching at the Gargoyle Club:

> I was having lunch with two Belgian journalists when a buzz bomb stopped overhead. No one else stopped eating. The Belgians, who were not fools, took one look at the glass walls and went under the table. I suspect that everyone else wanted to, but there was a kind of noblesse oblige about it. One feared more than anything else being embarrassed in front of the others.

Settle describes another occasion when, at the Albert Hall, although hearing the feared cut-out of a V1 engine overhead, the audience remained silently intent on a quiet Mozart cadence as the bomb plummeted down to explode a hundred yards away in Kensington Gardens.

At least you could hear the V1s coming. As an early form of ballistic missile the vastly more powerful V2s were entirely different. Descending from heights of fifty miles or more up in the stratosphere they travelled at many times the speed of sound and landed without warning; if you heard the explosion you were safe. Yet in one respect they were the same: they brought to London sudden, pointless death; inflicted entirely at random. It was brutal and exhausting.

At least people talked to each other. Traditional English reserve was largely sidelined by shared hardship. As Mary Lee Settle wrote, it was 'as if our statements had to be made before it was too late.' As those who lived through it remember, people encouraged each other with humour, understanding and sympathy for 'we were all in it together' – the war left no one untouched.

Season of Goodwill

The three or four letters a week that Hilda received from Ed were now not typed but handwritten from his bunk in the evenings: the H.Q. office was a lot busier than Leiston and the boss did not approve of time or machines being used for personal communication. Equally, telephone calls were now quick exchanges of information effected from a crowded room busy with voices and clattering typewriters, not relaxed conversations conducted from a lonely Nissen hut with a single buddy, if anyone, at the next desk. But dislocation and unfamiliarity with new surroundings served only to increase Ed's attachment to his girlfriend. He bought a leather-bound double picture frame for his desk and placed in it two pictures of Hilda, one a bare-shouldered glamour shot, the other an outdoor picture wearing a full-length coat. These attracted a lot of attention, not least from the senior officer in the PR section who suggested Hilda be immediately recruited as his personal civilian secretary. There was office debate on whether the bare-shouldered shot was appropriate: on balance the men thought that from Ed's point of view it was not, whereas the WACs thought it terrific. One captain was convinced that Ed was cheating; that he had obtained the photographs of some Hollywood starlet: he went on and on about it. Ed was proud and pleased and relayed all this sort of stuff to Hilda who, being a down-to-earth girl, had already tired a little of the gushing, unimpressed by hyperbole and romantic 'mush'.

Duties at High Wycombe might have been more demanding but weekends were usually free, allowing Ed to rendezvous with Hilda in London if she was not returning home to Knodishall. Anne's elder sister Mary had married an Englishman and now ran The Sugarloaf, a public house on Great Queen Street, close to Covent Garden market. It was a conveniently central meeting place for two people who enjoyed drinking and socialising. Weekends became long parties with the beautiful, laughing Hilda always at the centre. Everybody seemed to love her, even the girls.

In late November some of the old buddies from the Leiston base came down to join in the fun. On the Saturday morning Ed went off alone in search of a tailor to repair a revealing rip in the seat of his trousers. Behind a narrow shopfront near Holborn Viaduct he found one prepared to carry out a 'while-you-wait' repair and was sitting wedged next to the glass counter, wrapped in a length of green baize for the sake of decency, when an Irish nurse came in to collect a coat. Within the cramped confines of the Dickensian shop it was only natural the three should engage in conversation and, once reunited with his trousers, it was only hospitable that Ed should offer to buy the nurse a drink in a nearby pub. Three large gins and three beers later life stories had been exchanged and the nurse had become emotional, explaining how she had been jilted by a Yank and yet how wonderful it was to be with another. At this point Ed decided it would be best to emphasise that his girlfriend was waiting for him. The nurse was gracious in her disappointment, but, just in case, scribbled her phone number on a scrap of paper and pressed it into Ed's breast pocket as he left to collect Hilda from The Sugarloaf for a lunch-time meeting with a newspaper friend on Fleet Street.

Later, in El Vinos, the friend, Jim Pringle, appeared accompanied by his batchelor brother-in-law who, from his accent, was clearly Irish. '*Ah,*' thought Ed, '*the nurse!*' and went off to telephone the number in his pocket, so recruiting the Irish girl to the sizeable gang that met up at The Sugarloaf that evening before heading off to the Paramount Ballroom and a subsequent pub-crawl. The group included another young woman encountered that day, a Russian war correspondent on temporary assignment in London and met in El Vino's. Hardened on vodka and front-line reporting, she later proved able to drink the Americans under the table. When the pubs all closed at 10.30pm the nurse enthusiastically led the raucous group to a bar she said she knew would be open, but when this turned out to be a gay club the men became anxious to leave. The party returned to the street, staggering a little, to search for a more conventional venue. But the darkness of the 'dim-out' still in force, unfamiliarity with London, and absence of sobriety, led to several of its members becoming separated and then lost, to eventually sleep in a variety of unplanned locations. Ed and Hilda managed to stay together and with the aid of a taxi arrived at the St James Hotel at which, earlier in the week, Ed had booked a room with twin beds.

After a relaxed start Sundays usually continued Saturday nights with lunchtime 'hair of the dog' sessions with friends, colleagues and new acquaintances. These could 'jolly' on until it was time for Hilda to get to King's Cross for the late train to St Albans. After seeing her off Ed would hurry to Paddington for the train that would return him to his shared barrack hut at High Wycombe. The timing was tight, frequently resulting in his missing the train and spending the night in a room at a the Red Cross Club in Russell Square.

On this particular November evening he was on time and found himself sharing a carriage with two middle-aged ladies who addressed him in French, having noticed he was carrying a copy of one of the new French newspapers that had appeared in Paris following liberation. After struggling out of the linguistic muddle that resulted it was revealed that one of the two ladies had lived in Sarawak for twenty years and had a seventeen-year-old son who was a naval cadet and would love to meet '*un Americain*'. To that end she had invited two GIs to lunch at her home near Oxford but, when they telephoned from a public telephone box to confirm arrangements, they had omitted to Press Button 'A'. As they could not therefore hear the Frenchwoman shouting at them to do so, the call was not connected and the men failed to appear. She was amazed at their stupidity, particularly as they were not farm boys but New Yorkers, until Ed explained that Buttons 'A' and 'B' did not exist in the American telephone system. Ed promised to join them and the son for dinner as soon as he was able.

Back at the PR office the senior officer was much taken with news of the female Russian journalist, particularly when he learnt that she was not of the heavy masculine stereotype but was young and pretty. As the Allies efficiently crushing Nazi forces in a rapid westward advance towards Berlin, the Russians were very much in favour. News of exactly how brutally efficient was that advance had not yet filtered through, and the officer thought it an excellent idea to encourage friendly liason by taking the girl up in the latest model B-17 to show off all its technical wizardry. His enthusiasm turned to disappointment when Ed realised he could not remember any significant contact details about her except that her name was Magda.

Later in the week Ed was surprised to receive a short handwritten letter from one of Hilda's friends at the factory in St Albans. It offered, tentatively, to return a heart-shaped pendant which Ed had given to Hilda at the St James that past weekend. The letter-writer, a girl called Patricia, had admired it and instantly Hilda had given it to her. It was of good quality, expensively bought in the West End and Patricia felt guiltily uncomfortable. Ed felt astonished and just a little worried at the possible significance of the event, but was not the type to attempt to retrieve a gift. Instead he wrote to Hilda that whatever she had decided was fine by him. Though smoothed over, the event was indicative of the unthinking generosity that in later years would not always result in the happy endings Hilda intended.

Eight months into the relationship this was not the first sign of difficulty. There had been the halting 'on-off' start of the spring when Hilda had rebuffed Ed's enthusiasm and, despite the happy rapprochement of late July, the affair was occasionally interrupted by a black mood settling briefly over one or other of the two participants. It was not really surprising given the circumstances, for there was a war on. Hilda had lost her much-loved brother aged only twenty-five, and roomed with his saddened widow. Her father was not a well man: never robust after the privations he had suffered in World War I, the hard graft of concrete shuttering during the new conflict had further weakened him. Tiny Florrie, still struggling to maintain authority in her own household, appeared increasingly frail. Then there was the shameful business of Clifford; the long shifts in the St Albans factory; the awful death, injury and destruction randomly inflicted by first the V1 and then the V2 flying bombs; and all against the drab, seemingly endless emotional and physical exhaustion of the war. In December Hilda replied to one of Ed's letters 'I just want to lie in the sun and sleep, safely, for days and days and days ...'

For his part, since the insecurities of childhood and teenage years, Ed had trailed a small black dog of depression. Usually his enthusiasm for life and people, his curiosity, the love of his job and, especially, his elation at having found Hilda, kept it safely comatose. When it stirred he, like Hilda, sought escape in drinking; but alcohol could be an unreliable friend, as able to induce irrational unpleasant-ries as to drown worries. It was to become a recurrent problem, but in December such occasional setbacks were submerged under the increasing tempo of good times at parties, restaurants, pubs and London shows in the weeks before Christmas.

Christmas was to be spent at Mill House. Bob Rosenthal wrote to Ed from New York inquiring Hilda's size in order to send a gift of the family firm's latest lingerie fashion. Any surprise was lost, as Ed thought it best to ask Hilda her exact measurements to avoid risk of a misfit. He explained that while his father had made such garments of high quality silk, they were now created from a new, superior material called rayon. As food supplies remained tightly control-led by rationing, Ed took care to supplement Florrie's Christmas resources with various 'goodies' from the PX stores at the High Wycombe base; tinned ham being a particularly desirable commod-ity, together with tinned peaches and pears from California. Russell Bloomfield managed to locate two fat cockerels from the village and gave both to Florrie but, given the advantage of Ed's support, Florrie felt the needs of others were greater than her own and she packaged them both up for the post, sending one to Anne who was returning to Ireland for the holiday, and the other to Anne's sister Mary at The Sugarloaf.

Despite Jack's absence, that last Christmas of the war went well. The little sitting room was decorated with homemade paper chains scissored from old magazines, and pine boughs cut from Aldringham Common substituted for a Christmas tree. Carol singers called on Christmas Eve. Charlie and Alice were in relaxed and happy mood. Clifford contributed to the number present as did Russell for much of the time, together with various others who called in to swell a party fuelled by abundant US provisioning and charged with goodwill toward the high-spirited young couple that illuminated it. The smitten Ed seemed to follow Hilda from room to room as a puppy clings to its master. There was great hilarity when Hilda shaved him publicly in the kitchen; when he was pressed to eat a pickled onion for the first time in his life; and when grumpy old Charlie Ablett next door at The Butcher's Arms was prevailed upon to sell them a gallon of beer delivered into a chamber pot. On the train back to London Hilda feigned horror and embarrassment when Ed produced from his pocket the electric razor she had given him for Christmas and began to shave in the crowded carriage. Then, deciding to respond with a mockery of his crude American manners, she took a toothbrush from her bag and began brushing her teeth.

Harry

There was an unpleasant surprise waiting for Ed back at High Wycombe. A new 'gung-ho' commander was insisting that, despite the darkness and the freezing snow, all base personnel, including the WACs, should be present on the parade ground each morning for a 6.30am roll-call to be followed by a march to the mess hall for breakfast. Over the previous few months military routines on the base had gradually relaxed, allowing conditions to edge a little closer to the relative comforts of civilian life. This had been particularly so for the professional specialists – such as the news correspond-ents in the PR office – who had largely been left to organise their own affairs. Not anymore, and nobody was very happy about it. The reality, which was not at first appreciated by those affected, was that across the Channel in Belgium the Allied advance was in trouble as it attempted to stem the German breakthrough in the Ardennes. Faced with heavy troop losses, the military command was preparing to mobilise non-combatants, requiring Ed and everybody else, from cooks to clerks, to submit to medical examination to determine suitability for the Front. But by the second week of January the German offensive had been broken and the danger had passed to allow, towards the end of the month, a very personal peril to appear to challenge Ed's future. Harry, Hilda's old boyfriend, returned to England with the Second Army.

Harry was anxious to meet Hilda to determine how things stood and, if possible, to build on their previous relationship: after all, the memory of her had sustained him through some difficult times. Hilda, to the contrary, was confident that it was all in the past and told Ed as much, but decency demanded she give Harry such news personally, and in affairs of the heart the participants knew the outcome could never be guaranteed. Ed was hoping that Harry had fallen in love with some girl or other met in the course of his service in North Africa, Italy or France, but as Hilda told him to his consternation 'an Englishman always comes home to marry, whatever he's been up to abroad.'

The meeting was set for the evening of Saturday 27 January in St Albans rather than London. The capital would have been easier for Harry but, though breezily confident, Hilda had not wanted to be too distant from the female support of old friends Anne and Agnes, just in case. Harry, on leave, came down from his family in Liverpool. Ed, too nervous to enjoy himself in London, decided to stay at High Wycombe for the weekend and was on tenterhooks.

The difficulty for Hilda was that she was still not completely sure about Ed. Not that she thought for a moment that he was anything other than completely genuine and sincere. Just a troubling feeling deep down that there was something not quite right; that perhaps she was moving too far away from her roots; that when all the excitement and romance had cleared, levels of understanding might not balance so easily. In other words, she was not sure she was in love. Ed had no such doubts, he was confident that this was *the* girl. Since the success of Christmas, the flow of 'sweet nothing' letters attempting to describe, with consistent hyperbole, the extent of his love increased to the near daily level of the previous April. Awareness of Harry's imminent homecoming may have had something to do with it, but clearly he was besotted with his girlfriend and everything about her: her beauty, her extrovert sociability, her gentle family and their simple home-life. He was sure his future lay with Hilda.

When Harry called at 130 Waverley Road early on Saturday evening, Hilda suggested they walk to the The Spotted Bull. Seated at a quiet table they moved through a nervous preamble, exchanging news of each other's families and talking of Hilda's work in the factory, before Harry asked 'And what of us?' Never one to flee the demands of sensitive situations, Hilda gently described the extent of her relationship with Ed, and with her first few words Harry realised the game was lost: he had already sensed it from the moment of their meeting. More from honour than hope he played a weak rearguard action repeating the old warnings of GI irresponsibility and the hazards of clashing cultures, and 'what of those left at home?' But both knew it was over. Subdued and wistful Harry walked Hilda home early. Anne and Agnes had gone out and so Hilda went to bed to lie awake considering her future. Somewhere she had harboured the unformed thought that something, however unlikely, might perhaps have happened with Harry to either alter or confirm the course unfolding before her, something that would have removed doubt. And that was what had happened. It was simply no contest. For a vivacious woman like Hilda the tired old world of dull Harry could hold no attraction over the new, glamorous world of educated, wealthy Ed, the man who spent much of each week penning letters declaring his love. Raised in the Depression and living through a long, debilitating war, Hilda was of necessity a pragmatist. That was that. In the morning she wrote to Ed to confirm that Harry was out of the picture. He was elated.

Breaking News

During March and April the press room at Eighth Air Force Headquarters was hectic with stories from the Fronts. After the temporary setback in the Ardennes over Christmas the British and Americans were now forging west and north towards the Rhine, while from the east the Russian armies were racing for Berlin. Over the East Anglian airfields the sky seemed permanently filled with the roar of heavy engines as endless formations of Fortresses and Liberators streamed out on thousand-bomber raids to pulverise German cities. Stories released to the civilian press and to military publications had to hit the correct balance between morale-boosting propaganda and factual news. Atrocities committed by the enemy, such as the German massacre of American prisoners at Malmedy in the Ardennes, were generally given factual, if edited, coverage, whereas occasional reports of Russian atrocities in the East were dismissed as German-originated propaganda. The terrible carnage inflicted on German civilians by the bombing campaign was also left largely unreported, though had it been fully disclosed little sympathy would have been likely amongst survivors of the Blitz. Any possible chance of empathy with German victims evaporated once reports arrived in London from the Belsen concentration camp after its liberation by the British 11th Armoured Division on 15 April.

Human interest stories were always popular. One that Ed relayed to Hilda was of a B-17 tail-gunner who, with his intercom inoperative, failed to receive the order to bale out after the aircraft was damaged by a German fighter over France. In the event the plane stabilised itself on auto-pilot and flew on across the Channel towards England, the tail-gunner unaware he was the only one of the ten-man crew left aboard. After using his guns to see off another fighter that briefly attacked he was over Devon before realising his situation and bailing out, leaving the aircraft to fly on unmanned until it ran out of fuel and crashed in Wales. The rest of the crew were taken prisoner by the Germans.

A frustration of working in a military press office was that after using his skills to write up a good story, Ed was obliged to submit the result for approval, not to a senior editor, but to a senior officer. As he complained to Hilda, any subsequent discussion was not resolved by the merit of the piece but by the views, and the superior rank, of the officer who was often not a professional newsman. In that context it was with particular relish that Ed enjoyed a visit to the office by Ernest Hemingway in early March.

With the successful *For Whom The Bell Tolls* published in 1940 and *A Farewell To Arms* just made into a popular motion picture, Hemingway was a significant celebrity and came into the office escorted by the senior PR officer and a number of high-ranking Eighth Air Force men including the base commander. As the great novelist's eyes met Ed's he recognised the young reporter from the San Francisco *Call-Bulletin* who had interviewed him before the war. A friendly conversation followed to the surprise of the officers and to the delight of Ed whose professional kudos was being so publicly boosted. Whether connected to the Hemingway incident or not, news arrived the same week that Ed was to be promoted to sergeant.

His advance continued unchecked with the US Army magazine *Yank* commissioning him to provide an article on the 357th Fighter Group at the Leiston base. The boys at his old home were achieving fame as the most successful Fighter Group in the Eighth Air Force. The story was well received and a request followed for a longer article covering the whole of the Eighth Air Force campaign in Europe. Then the Forces newspaper *Stars and Stripes* requested Ed be seconded to their European operation and, if that was not enough, conversations with Jim Pringle and others on Fleet Street implied that a job with United Press in London was assured once the war ended. In mid-March news broke that the Russians had taken Kuestrin, a bare thirty miles from Berlin, and it seemed that peace was in sight.

With the potential difficulty of Harry removed, the romance was also fast-moving. The Kentish seaside town of Rye was recommended by one of Ed's hut-mates as an excellent location for a quiet weekend away with Hilda: the sort of cosy place where plans could be discussed and commitments made. It was also reported as one of the few towns on the south coast largely free of noisy GIs. The visit was made and the following weekend Ed once again waited nervously at High Wycombe as Hilda travelled alone to Mill House to announce her intention of marrying. It was almost exactly a year since the meeting in The Volunteer.

Inspection and Approval

George and Florrie had anticipated the announcement; it was more confirmation than news. They were quietly pleased, for Ed was a popular addition to the household. He was testament to the easy-going friendliness and generosity that had so marked the American 'invasion' but more than that they could sense the sincerity of his affection for Hilda, and for themselves. The happy news of the engagement served also as counterweight to the anniversary of the fearful night when the *Mahratta* had gone down with such loss of young life. Still Florrie hoped against the odds. On 21 February she had written to Anne 'I pray and trust it will be God's will to bring our Jack safe back home'. In Florrie's case it was not so much a conspiracy of denial as an awareness that in the uncertainty of war anything could happen.

Many proposed GI weddings met with disapproval from parents who considered American exuberance uncouth and vulgar. They foresaw, often correctly, problems with cultural differences. Mothers, though perhaps sympathetic to the romance, could be reluctant to lose a daughter overseas, particularly if, like Florrie, they had lost a son. But Ed need not have feared; George was no family autocrat but a gentle soul who had not inherited the dominating ways of his mother. In any event he was very fond of Eddie who, when he had been at the Leiston base, used to call at Mill House, even if he knew Hilda was not at home, for a chat or a pint with George at The Butcher's. Florrie's first concern was for the happiness of their

remaining child. And both parents knew their daughter was sufficiently headstrong to do what she thought best, whatever advice or
opinion might be offered. Happy for Hilda, they were further pleased,
and relieved, when she explained that it seemed unlikely she and Ed
would live in the US after the war as Ed was hoping to find work
in London, or perhaps Paris, so she would never be too far away for
frequent visits. The only immediate problem was that with the war in
the Pacific predicted not to end until late 1946, their was a possibility
that Ed might be transferred to that theatre of operations before a
wedding could be arranged.

Once released, news of the coming marriage prompted warnings,
inspections and approvals, local and international. Letters of congrat-
ulation arrived at High Wycombe from family and friends. One was
from elder brother Larry containing the announcement that he was
taking leave from his base on the Clyde to come down to London
to meet Hilda over the weekend of 17 March. It was his first visit
to the capital so, taking command of the threesome, he insisted on
a comprehensive tour entirely on foot. Ed recorded his exhaustion
in the following week's letters to Hilda. As eldest son and successful Wall Street lawyer, Larry was known to occasionally assume a
mantle of seniority in the presence of his brothers who, perceiving
condescension, could react with irritation. But the London visit
went well; there were no fraternal arguments and, as expected, Larry
found Hilda delightful, reporting back to the family on Long Island
'Beautiful she is, and everything a man could want, but relax – her
hair ain't like heather!'

Ed had no sooner returned to High Wycombe after seeing Larry
off on the train back to Glasgow than a phone call came through
announcing another 'inspection'. The call was from Celia Simon,
one of his San Francisco friends, just posted to London as a Red
Cross hostess. She was anxious to meet Hilda, claiming that the gang
in California had despatched her to England specifically to vet the
prospective Mrs Rosenthal as there was a fear in San Francisco that
Ed might be suffering from some kind of war fatigue and had lost
his powers of judgement. In due course she too wrote back saying

'Forget your worries, I don't know how he's done it but Ed has hit the jack-pot!'

Then came the warning and a threat. Enclosed with a letter from Hilda, Ed received a short note signed by both Agnes and Anne. It said that should news ever reach their ears that he had been anything other than loving, considerate and generous towards Hilda they, with physical back-up from Eric, would track him down wherever he tried to hide and leave him unable to ever consider romance again. Eric was unable to sign as after assisting with cross-Channel *Pluto* operations through the summer and autumn, he had been sent to the Solomon Islands to assist the Americans with training for amphibious assault. The Americans, having taken Guadalcanal and several other fiercely contested islands, felt in no need of instruction from the British, leaving Eric with little to do except swim in the warm seas and dream of returning home to marry Agnes.

The approval Ed most required for marriage while still enrolled in the army was that of his commanding officer. Regulations stipulated the prerequisite was interview and preliminary approval by the base chaplain. Ed was indignant, writing to Hilda on 19 April to say he felt it 'damned impertinent to be treated as a couple of under-age kids rushing into marriage without due consideration.' That, of course, was exactly what the process was designed to prevent, under the broader policy of generally discouraging servicemen from marrying abroad. It was also intended to uncover any aspiring brides or grooms with disingenuous motives, and rules had to be applied without exception. Consequently Hilda was obliged to join Ed at Eighth Air Force Headquarters to submit to searching questions from the chaplain, a southerner from the Alabama 'Bible Belt'. After briefly querying Ed on his service record and future plans he addressed Hilda: 'Ah understand ya want to marry this soldier?'

'Yes, I do.'

'And why do ya wanna do that?'

'I love him.'

'And are ya expecting child?' asked the chaplain, reading from a mental script.

'Definitely not!' responded Hilda as Ed opened his mouth to object.
'Then Ah can recommend that military approval for this marriage
be given right away – congratulations to ya both!' and the interview
was over.

Occupation

On 30 April Hitler shot himself in the bunker below the Reich
Chancellery in Berlin and over the following week the remnants of
the German forces surrendered to the Allies. Victory in Europe was
officially announced on 8 May and England exploded in celebration
and relief. That night in St Albans bonfires blazed in the rejoicing but
Ed could not find Hilda in the surrounding darkness. Overwhelmed
by the significance of the occasion she had withdrawn from the singing and the drinking to be alone. At twenty-four, the six years of war
had dominated her young life. She had lived through some of the
darkest days in the country's history. She had lost a brother, met a
husband and lived a life that at eighteen in Knodishall she could never
have imagined. Now she stood on the cusp of something new and
unfamiliar and perhaps just as daunting, a peacetime marriage to an
American. She wanted time alone to reflect on what had passed and
what was beginning. Agnes was annoyed, complaining to Ed 'Hilda
should be with us now!' but Ed understood. Hilda might have been
the life and soul of a party but sometimes her gaze would pass over the
immediate frenzy and settle quietly on something more profound.

At the beginning of June Ed was sent to Germany to report from
the occupying US Army. Setting off from Cherbourg in an army Jeep
with two fellow pressmen, he got no further than Paris before the
engine seized, obliging him to spend four days in the city waiting
for army mechanics to effect repairs. The visit provided the realisation that the mooted Paris posting with *Stars and Stripes* might be an
attractive proposition. His two companions were to remain in the
French capital, leaving Ed to drive on alone eastward into Germany.
He first visited the ruins of Frankfurt before deciding to file a story

from Hitler's spectacular Alpine headquarters, 'The Eagle's Nest'. Situated close to the old family home at Bad Nauheim this choice might have been influenced by a desire to visit his roots, though given the circumstances, he professed little inclination to search for connections. He found the small spa town undamaged and beautiful, and inevitably his curiosity got the better of any wish to stand apart. With his identity and origins revealed to the barkeepers of the town's hostelries, friends and acquaintances of his father's family made themselves known; any relatives who might have been present before the war had long since fled, or had gone to the ovens. Regrets were expressed, many most likely sincere, but Ed was unforgiving; moving on to the town of Gotha he wrote to Hilda from US Army Headquarters in the Hotel Stadt Coburg on a requisitioned German typewriter 'NOW they are sorry. Well, it's just too late!'

His anger had not dissipated by the time he reached Hamburg. In an article later published in the English magazine *Illustrated* he dwelt on the reaction of Germans reminded of Nazi horrors. The article opened by recounting an interview conducted with a Hamburg civilian who had worked in New York in the 1930s and was hoping to find work as an interpreter with the occupying forces.

> The German leaned forward with a fierce intensity. 'I didn't want to join the [Nazi] Party' he insisted in rusty English. 'It was that … that I was helpless. As soon as I got back my wife told me not to talk loudly when I said things against the Nazis. At first I couldn't understand.'
>
> I said bluntly 'Throughout the war we always thought there was one kind of good German'.
>
> His bony features brightened 'I knew you Americans would understand.'
>
> 'That's not what I mean.'
>
> 'No?' he eyed me strangely 'Then what kind of good German do you mean?'
>
> 'A dead one!' I snapped.

That the full horror of the final months of the war in Germany had yet to be revealed was indicated by this article, in accord with the received wisdom of the day, discounting stories of Russian atrocities as being no more than German propaganda.

From Hamburg Ed wrote to Hilda on 10 June to describe what he had found: square miles of house-high rubble fields shot through with the curled steel of twisted girders. Here and there in the flattened city the empty shell of a blasted building rose from the devastation as if on a stage set for the final apocalypse. Yet in the outlying suburbs he reported little damage amongst the rows of comfortable villas except for the occasional fire-blackened ruin where a stray incendiary had done its worst. He was billeted in a luxurious house 'liberated' from a wealthy businessman with each soldier enjoying the near-forgotten novelty of an individual room equipped with its own bathroom. Several large German staff cars had been requisitioned to tour the city, together with a naval launch that allowed Ed to inspect the wharves of a harbour littered with sunken vessels and floating detritus which, he remembered later, included the rotting corpse of a small brown dog.

Something Borrowed

As Ed toured the devastation in Germany, Agnes went into the centre of St Albans with Hilda in search of a wedding dress; Eric was on a ship on his way back from the Pacific and the wedding was planned for the end of the month. As Agnes earned a good deal more on the buses than Hilda did in the electronics factory the arrangement was that Agnes would buy the dress with her Post Office savings and later loan it to Hilda who had no savings. Hilda, having perused what was available in the stores of the West End in the enabling company of Ed, encouraged Agnes to go for the best she could afford and, after a morning of fun and giggles, a traditional style in white silk was purchased. On 30 June Agnes wore it to the Catholic church of St Stephen where it set off the dark blue of Eric's uniform to perfection.

Exactly a week later, on 7 July 1945, Hilda Vera Thorpe of Mill House, Knodishall wore it for her marriage to Staff Sergeant Edwin

S. Rosenthal of California. The ceremony took place at 2pm at the Church of St Lawrence, Knodishall and the reception was held at the Legion Hut just across the Common from Mill House. The old buddies from the airfield, or at least those who were still there, were invited together with everyone who knew Hilda, which meant that the event soon became an open-house for all in the village. Hilda was Knodishall's first GI bride and the Stars and Stripes flew with the Union Jack on the flagpole. Old men today can remember that occasion when, as small boys, they were confronted by more food and drink than they had ever seen in their lives before. By coincidence it was on the very next day that the 357th Fighter Group completed its departure from Leiston for a base near Munich. Suddenly it was all over. The great expanse of airfield and its scattered township lay empty and silent. A week afterwards, when Hilda returned from honeymoon in the Scilly Isles, Agnes was only a little surprised to discover that she had given away the wedding dress to someone she felt needed it more. 'After all,' Hilda explained 'we're married now.'

May 2003

The sound came before any visual contact, a deep droning, difficult to locate. Many in the crowd raised flattened hands to their foreheads to scan the banks of dark cloud building from the west. Then the sun flashed shining on bright wing metal and several voices spoke together 'There he is!' The Mustang banked right to align with where the old runway had been, levelled, and streaked over the green wheat just above the telephone poles, the pilot's head silhouetted through the perspex of the cockpit canopy. Just past the crowd he pulled the nose skyward and with a growl of engine noise climbed vertically to 10,000 feet in a second or two. Now the size of a bee lost in the cloud he rolled the aircraft ready for the descent. The sound was unfamiliar, not the ear-splitting shriek or deafening roar of a modern jet, nor the high-revving scream of a motorcycle. It was the deeper, slower sound of a big-bored petrol engine and, like the aircraft itself, seemed more manageable, friendlier, more human in scale. To one or two in the crowd it brought a lump to the throat.

The occasion was the commemoration of the arrival of the Americans at Leiston, Station F373 sixty years earlier. The participants stood by a small memorial near the southern end of what had been the main runway. One, Merle Olmsted, had served here. Many of the others had hung around the base as schoolboys befriending the Yanks and scavenging for perspex from wrecked aircraft to carve into rings. They had been at the children's parties put on by the Americans and, like the young women, would never forget the excitement and lavish hospitality. But many of the onlookers were much younger, men and women born after the war. What happened six decades ago that continues to so enthral two and three generations?

The tidal wave of Americans that swamped Suffolk between 1942 and 1945 will remain unique in its impact. Swamped is not too strong a word: at the time Leiston, itself unique as a small industrial town in a rural county, had a population of about 4,000. The purely agricultural areas surrounding other bases such as nearby Parham held far fewer people. By contrast the airfields each accommodated 1,500–3,000 US servicemen. Now global communication and commerce has carried American influence to even the remotest communities, with the result that western societies, at least, are increasingly homogenised. Sixty years ago rural life in Suffolk had more in common with Elizabethan society than American: the Yanks might have been from Mars.

Inevitably there was conflict. The higher pay of the GIs, their noisy exuberance which many interpreted as cocky arrogance, their profligacy with food and fuel despite domestic shortages and, especially, their voracious appetite for English girls, often reciprocated, all caused resentment. After the war the writer Harold Nicolson voiced his displeasure that 'the destinies of the world should be in the hands of a giant with the limbs of an undergraduate, the emotions of a spinster and the brains of a peahen.' Similar views survive in Europe today as the actions of the remaining superpower are likened to the flailings of a giant – over-consumptive of resources and under-endowed with wisdom. Equally it was true that many GIs viewed the British as the enervated, backward and dirty inhabitants of a crumbling, class-ridden society. To some Leiston was a freezing mud-hole, to be left behind as a bad memory as soon as a tour of duty could be completed.

Prejudice on both sides evaporated wherever friendly interaction occurred at a personal level. Some 50,000 of these interactions resulted in GI brides, the majority moving to the US – the ebb tide of the GI occupation. These marriages, together with the friendships made during the hard times of war, created a network of transatlantic links which, tenuous at first, strengthened with the improving post-war economy and the increasing mobility of ordinary people. In itself the GI occupation did not trigger a sudden post-war Americanisation of Britain, either psychologically or commercially. Rather it was a small step in a process that accelerated under the influence of international US commercialism in an increasingly affluent post-war society.

The most profound legacy of those few years in the 1940s are memories. The memories of people struggling together through a time when the world stood trembling between light and dark and the young of both sides held the front lines. Ed's excitement at being party to the brushstrokes of history was perceptive. In that respect the significance of those days has not been lost on those who lived them, nor on their descendants. For the first group memories are etched deep of comradeship and irrepressible good humour in the face of death, destruction and hardship. For the second the realisation that such relatively recent times, so pivotal to the course of modern history, are about to slip from living memory has fired both a hunger to know more of them and an appetite for their nostalgia. That is why some two hundred people stand in a Suffolk field at an unpublicised event to watch an old aircraft fly low over a vanished runway. But it was for those who were young and in love that the memories are most intense; memories of dance and music and romance, shaking youth free from the old pre-war restraints. That is why Hilda kept and carefully filed all the letters she received from her American, and why that American, divorced and remarried, would never talk of those years.

Bibliography

Primary Sources:

Letters (mainly undated) written by Ed Rosenthal to his family during the period 1934–1945.

Letters written by Ed Rosenthal to Hilda Thorpe 15.03.44 to 10.06.45

Letters written by Ed Rosenthal to Robert Rosenthal 30.10.80 to 28.09.81

Interviews with Suffolk residents conducted by author 2003 to 2007 (see Acknowledgements).

Letter to author from Robert Rosenthal 18.07.03

Thorpe family correspondence 1941–1945 including letter from Royal Naval Barracks, Devonport 19.01.42 and telegrams

Private documents Thorpe/Rosenthal: birth and marriage certificates etc.

Various newspaper cuttings 1935–1944

Yank magazine 18.05.45

Illustrated magazine 29.05.45

Discussion and telephone conversations with family members. Oral family history known to author

Family photographs

Secondary Sources:

Banham, Tony *Not the Slightest Chance* (Hong Kong: Hong Kong University Press, 2003)

Bowman, Martin W. *Wild Blue Yonder* (London: Cassell, 2003)

Cooke, Alistair *Alistair Cooke's America* (London: BBC, 1973)

Crosby, Harry H. *A Wing and a Prayer* (London: Robson Books, 1993)

Dewing, Geoff *Aldeburgh 1939–1945* (Surrey: privately published, 1995)

Freeman, Roger A. *The Mighty Eighth* (London: Military Book Society, 1970)

F.O.L.A. *Leiston, Memories of a Suffolk Airfield* (Leiston: privately published, 2002)

Guest, Freddie *Escape from the Bloodied Sun* (London: Jarrolds, 1956)

Longmate, Norman *The G.I.s. The Americans in Britain 1942–1945* (London: Hutchinson, 1975)

Jobson, Allan *Suffolk Yesterdays* (London: Heath Cranton, 1944)

Lamb, Andrea *The Americans in Parham* (unpublished dissertation, Parham Airfield Museum 1999)

May, D.Y. & K. *From Flint Knappers to Atom Splitters* (Leiston: Quickthorn Books, 2001)

Millgate, Helen D. *Got Any Gum Chum? G.I.s in Wartime Britain 1942–1945* (Stroud: Sutton Publishing, 2001)

Ogilvie de Mille, Ailsa *One Man's Dream: Thorpeness* (Dereham: Nostalgia Publications, 1996)

Reilly, Terry *Dear Old Ballina* (Ballina: privately published, 1993)

Reynolds, David *Rich Relations. The American Occupation of Britain 1942–1945* (London: HarperCollins, 1995)

Snow, Philip *The Fall of Hong Kong* (New Haven: Yale University Press, 2003)

Way, Chris *Glenn Miller in Britain, Then and Now* (London: After the Battle, 1996)

Whitehead, R.A. *Garrett 200* (London: Transport Bookman, 1978)

Winfield, Pamela *Melancholy Baby* (Westport, CT: Bergin and Garvey, 2000)

Woodman, Richard *Arctic Convoys 1941–1945* (London: John Murray, 1994)

Internet resources particularly mwadui.com (Richard Hide) ref. Hong Kong escape
vqronline.org ref. Mary Lee Settle
newsquest.co.uk and uboat.net ref. HMS *Mahratta*

Index